THE SLASHER AND THE VAMPIRE AS ROLE MODELS
New & Selected Poems

IAN GREGSON

Published by Cinnamon Press
Meirion House
Tanygrisiau
Blaenau Ffestiniog
Gwynedd, LL41 3SU
www.cinnamonpress.com

The right of Ian Gregson to be identified as author of this work has been asserted by him in accordance with the Copyright, Designs and Patent Act, 1988. Copyright © 2020 Ian Gregson.
ISBN: 978-1-78864-068-8
British Library Cataloguing in Publication Data. A CIP record for this book can be obtained from the British Library.
All rights reserved. No part of this publication may be reproduced, stored in a retrieval system, or transmitted in any form or by any means, electronic, mechanical, photocopying, recording or otherwise without the prior written permission of the publishers. This book may not be lent, hired out, resold or otherwise disposed of by way of trade in any form of binding or cover other than that in which it is published, without the prior consent of the publishers.
Designed and typeset in Palatino by Cinnamon Press.
Cover design by Adam Craig.
Cinnamon Press is represented in the UK by Inpress Ltd and in Wales by the Welsh Books Council.
Cinnamon Press acknowledges the financial support of the Books Council of Wales.

Acknowledgements

Poems from *Call Centre Love Song* first published in *Call Centre Love Song*, Salt Publishing, 2006. Poems from *How We Met* first published in *How We Met*, Salt Publishing, 2008.
Some of the poems included here were previously published in the following periodicals:
Agenda, Endymion, Envoi, The Independent, The Forward Book of Poetry 2007, The Gregory Awards 1980 and 1981-2, The Jacaranda Review, The London Review of Books, The New Welsh Review, The North, Planet, Poetry Review, Poetry Wales, The Rialto, Stand, The Times, and *The Times Literary Supplement.*
'The Great Escape' was the subject of one of Frieda Hughes's columns in *The Times.*
'Squawks and Speech' was a *Guardian* Poem of the Week.

Contents

Selected Poems

From *Call Centre Love Song*:

txt	11
Call Centre Love Song	12
How I Invented Sex	14
That Change	16
The Personals	18
The Roof	20
Someone to Watch Over You	22
A Foreign Body	24
my husband is an alien—	28
A Professional Worrier	26
I'm English, and wicked	30
The Adman's Breakdown	32
Boggart Holes	34
How Does It Feel?	35
Parys Mountain 1	38
Parys Mountain 2	39
Phallic Shit	40
Freeze Frame	42
A Coypu	43
The Great Escape	44
The Breakwater	45
in the twin city	46
Animations	48
Why I'm Too Cowardly to Have a Vasectomy	50
Deconstructionists on Fast Forward	52
Shadowing	53
Thomas the Tank Engine Reaches Puberty	56
The Hawk at the Shrink	58
Voice Over	60
Fast Asleep	62
Fast Asleep Too	63
Elusive Boy	64

Carriers of the End	67
Following the Charts	68
The Creature from the Black Lagoon (U.S. 1952)	69
Vengeance is Mine	70
The Vicar and the Rag and Bone Man	72
Happy the Man	73
A Dislocation	74
The Sick Room	75
A Dental Appointment	76
Her Mother's Way	77
From Whose Bourn	78
In the New House	80
The Smaller Picture	81
Superman and Lois	82
The Café Bar of Rejection	92
Fully Explained	93
Saturday Night Revisited	94
For in the Picture Sat a Plywood Gap	96
Undercurrents of Easter	98
Sultry	99

From *How We Met*:

It could be love	103
Sideways at the War	104
The Scaremonger	106
Postmodernism, Or,	107
Grey Areas	108
Squawks and Speech	110
Folie à Deux	112
Fallen Women #1–7	113
Misconceiving	114
Surface Impressions	116
Crab Lane From the New Flats	118
How We Met	119
The William Ewart Gladstone Comic Strip	
Part One: The Medium	136
Part Two: The Strips	141

New Poems:

Heartbreak Hotel:

Foreign Bodies	177
Heartbreak Hotel	178
Croeso ar Fwrdd Coastliner Cymru	179
The Housekeeper	180
Lucky Pierre	181
Desirable Residence	182
Dolgarrog Flood, 1925	183
The Hearing Aid	184
The Older Sister	185
Shrieking Halyards	186
Mundane	187
World of Interiors	188
Box of Vision	189
The Breasts	190
Emily Dickinson Updates Her Facebook Status	191
Spar Radio	192
The Cu Chi Tunnels	193
The Stuffing Boxes	194
The Prison of Memory, 1989	195
Breaking the Ice	196
The Gold Bar	197
Sports Psychology	198
Muntjak	199
Fluent	200
Glass Houses	201
Socialism for the Rich	202

The Slasher and the Vampire as Role Models

You Faithless Slime	205
Outlaws	206
Major Lawrence	208
Being Requited	210

The Living Dead	212
A Police Officer Called Marilyn	213
A Dentist's Jane Austen	216
Meg Ryan	218
The Porter and the Slasher	219
Off the Road	220
Bishop Shoots Brando	222
The Process	223
The Familiar	224
The Foreign Secretary Circles the Wagons	226
Unearthly Hour	228

The Slasher and the Vampire as Role Models

For Ceri

From *Call Centre Love Song*

txt

since yr remve
i hav 2 send

u these
lke sand

letters the c
silences

lke i am def
wanting 2

sign in the dark
scrawl on yr hand

lke smthng
lost frm lve

Call Centre Love Song

I'm edgy now with looming blame.
To fall in love with just a voice!
You asked for me again by name
And boggled my poise like secret vice.

My office runs a strict regime.
Be *this* I'm told, and then I *am* it,
losing myself to please the team.
It's hectic at *Exotic Planet*.

We answer calls. The room is cramped —
too many screens like twitchy pools.
You talk as though you're free, exempt
from all restrictive rules.

I hate myself that I'm compliant:
Eight Reasons For Leaving Your Desk,
and none is loving a client.
You booked our *Scorching Arabesque*:

I pictured you riding a camel
piercing sandstorms in a blue burnous.
We've never met. It isn't normal
to feel your absence in my mouse:

it aches to call you up on screen
and give your name a cyber-face
and show me where and how you've been.
But nothing could erase

the gulf between us made of money.
You whisper your thousands in my ear
which stresses my lack of any,
and niggles my hope like sudden fear

and stiffens my finger on my mouse.
A hundred calls are stuck on hold
all listening to Johann Strauss.
I'm rigidly controlled

as though I'm trapped inside a screen
and made to picture all I'm told
and flicker with scene after scene
then empty like a pane gone cold

as the sun withdraws from its glass;
or like a mobile dropped in a squall
of voices in an underpass
that frailly repeats its lost call.

How I Invented Sex

Something beyond just planting seed,
something in a range of styles,
huge it was, this need.
More an explosion waiting, and our trials
revealed *Cool Sex* could spark it.
Huge it was, the gap in the market.

I spoke one morning to a guinea pig.
She'd waited for this forever:
like being suspended from a peg
and the wet ripples across her running all over
twisting inside out with the big
breeze that was flooding through her as she shook
in answer to the old need, and came unstuck,
hurtling away in the huge weather.

We could supply the lack
like the housewife wanted.
                        More,
our subjects fill up with fulfilment 'til they leak
out of themselves and out of before
into an after quiet, amazed, only slightly sore.

Thousands found themselves, through my technique,
reborn as virtuosi,
stars of erotic chic.
Others stayed beginners.
We needed losers as well as winners
who make it seem so easy
their feelings feel unique.

So quickly and so much!
And the climb so steep and so dizzy
I looked into myself like vertigo
and flared up like a match.

I cut a record, published a book
and hosted my weekly game show
Can't Fuck, Won't Fuck
to put more millions in the know
and get more millions to compete
and try to enter our élite...

I grew so big and armoured with control
and knowing fully how to be,
as though the world's a vast keyhole
and only I
could stroll towards it with the key.

That Change

The autumn afternoon he crawled about that damp pavement—
his second wife relives it now, as often before:

small stones that poked his knees and palms and briefly clung,
the not believing that change like from nowhere a slap—

the change that was taking hold as his lunch-hour lengthened
into hours where an urgent meeting should've been.

She can smell the exhaust where the dark tube breathed on him
and feel the grey-on-grey hard stipple of the paving,

see the mostly curving thin cracks in broken paving,
cracks *between* paving, grown with scuffed moss

at the furthest edge of his first marriage

where his tight routine slackened around his bar table
with its overflowing ashtray and turned-off mobile

and he was thinking of her, his second wife to be
who waits for him in the autumn evening four years later:

How many times must a man be made to realise
as then he must've done—as though he could feel for the first time

his ankles and knees, his palms and fingers—
what moves in him below his neck?

She can feel the traffic thrum in his fingers and knees,
in the subculture of dogs and ankles,

his second striped and longer tongue licking the cracks,
the gnarled and pitted kerbs, while voices and expressions

broke in waves above his head, dispersing
as he swam through the street towards their new life.

But all around her the darkness deepens and wonders:

Couldn't another change now start in him
out of her reach, so that his knees

fall to his knees, a change like an unsuspected place
surprising his fingers, boggling his eyes?

The Personals

I'll choose two people from this page—
one to want and one to be
all made up from those words, an age
and status, how to look and see
all unlike the who
I must be always being,
an I to fit a You—
send myself like a message:
cerebral but funny, leftish but skiing.

So many characters
in search of a plot,
so many futures waiting to happen
which to me will not—
cultured and wild, a Venus against furs:
such futures, on this page, open
where mine is married, mortgaged, shut—
to know who to want, and what *for*,
searching for Love, or nearest offer,

pose myself like a question
and watch the blond muscular answer—
tall and thirty, open to suggestion-
stroll towards my table
thinking *eco-anxious, sinuous dancer*
thinking *sporty, busty, fun,*
feeling a wish grow palpable,
doing all I've never done
and seeing the ghost of the possible

who slipped out of sight
where facing windows treble the light
and his figure that broke
and flickered—perfect match,
a partner bespoke:
nervous, unstable, bright
but lost by the bridge, the building-site,
park railings or subway, who glimpses catch
fitful as a shadow on a watch

but might be conjured by this spell:
my age and status, how I look and see—
but no.
I'll make these types my proxies,
make them meet like parts of me
where column inches lengthen and spill
knowing the pleasure of both sexes—
shrunk to a few words, then born anew
and stuffed through millions of letter boxes.

The Roof

A fortnight after my husband left for good
damp patches flowered on my bedroom wallpaper.

A handsome bald broad-shouldered man climbed from his van
and nodded at my roof:I needed urgent surgery.

A pretty boy, his son, with a nose-ring, and Bob
built to the sound of music scaffolding
like a skeleton worn fashionably on the outside.

Their DJ echoed from somewhere like a voice that slipped
inside me next to my thinking—also news, and sport.

Their hammers cut into the heavy slate
then deepened and undid the raftered skull

opening the soft pine until the splinters
showered through the skeleton and dust misted the windows.

Torn felt, long slats of furry wood with rusty nails,
broken slates and plaster heaped up in the garden from their dig:

my bed was empty but they were unearthing overhead
a lost storey of music and shouts and heavy steps,

my doors were open front and back to street noises
and they sang and danced around my kids on dusty boots.

The looks of passers-by all climbed the scaffolding
and entered where the secret was unfolding—

I minded at first the new exposure
then I didn't, and the next morning

rain was falling through me
but there were dry patches on the road under the cars

and humming hands cradled and rocked a skip
down to the road.Then overnight the street all joined

the purging with me: added to my soiled slate
a kettle, legless doll, damp shreds of thick wallpaper

Someone to Watch Over You

Sometimes I think myself so near to you
almost you might feel my breath
stir your hair

hover and hover but never appear to you
like your lover after his death
lingering where

you speak to me but I can never reply
and yet I can never go
held by the force

sticking your face like a freeze-frame in my eye
pushing me to need to know
all that's yours

slipping that day through your kitchen window
stepping one trainer on your unit
jumping free

into your flat that says you need me to mind you
danger might surface any minute
telepathy

lets me feel your craving like a tune both of us hum
together though we're miles apart
absences

live in your bedroom like an arm that's grown numb
so the pumped-up luminous heart
yellow dress

single rose
I leave waiting to open
clues like *Killing Me Softly* sung on your ansaphone

mementoes
of something lying in wait to happen
where each detail of you would be thoroughly known

like a star
living for me in my cuttings
taped undressings shreds of clothing locks of hair

near but far
always please and scattered in things
and not fixed and nowhere at once and everywhere

A Foreign Body

Forces are secretly working
unknown to camera crews:
what flickers in my living-room
floats on the surface of news.

Insiders watch the forms all cloudy
blurred in the distance looming,
knowing already how they'll sharpen,
aiming their cameras and zooming.

But what the news had said was true
is over like a fiction:
all I had relied on growing up
like *mutually assured destruction*.

The changes happen behind my back,
I turn the corner shaken—
changed myself in secret but sure
the landscape is mistaken.

The forces in hiding will collide
and mix their DNA—
in Africa somewhere or the East—
and start to head this way.

I see a picture briefly, say,
from Russia: movement caught
in the corner of my sleepy eye—
some bar, some bank, some port.

This picture conspires with others,
forcing, by freak, a merger:
I'm not looking that way at all
and yet the picture's growing larger.

The foreign body I inhale
has travelled half the planet:
it's nothing to do with me
until I find I *am* it.

I step out of a future mirror
wondering what I want.
I walk towards me like a threat
and wear myself back to front.

my husband is an alien—

else why ignore the baby and me
up in his study or down in his shed
with the light all shrivelled from his face.
Like finding a different way to be
dictated by the spider in his head,
the old him gone and filled up with space—

at least since he lost his job.
Time stuns him and deepens like space
and he suffers the house like a shock
and lives all day at his club
and something else is looking through his face.
He's lost to himself like a sock

stretched out on a beach on its own
growing foreign to his own moods.
He's silent like listening in
to strangers plotting on the phone,
and walks his secret paths in the woods
forgetting how to be who he's been.

The day we watched the baby on the screen
floating in its monochrome
outlandish capsule, something got
into him, like fishing, golf—whatever would mean
(metal detection!) he'd be not at home,
but deep into headphones on his yacht

and the voices of weather and shipping,
all away from broody me who swells
and looks all day inside, inside
to where this force, not me, unzipping
my self, has planted something else
and where I grow so fully occupied—

while he's, in all the wrong ways, a new man
searching the suburbs for a new frontier,
and maps, statistics, like an alien spy
reporting what it is to be human
from the outside, like a pioneer
staring at patterns in the night sky

and itching to launch his pointy probe,
but also secretive and bound
tight inside himself where he's concealed
like condoms inside a globe:
deep into headphones hoovering a field,
listening for messages from underground.

A Professional Worrier

Official title: worry surrogate.

I noticed the Power first when Steve my best mate
was frantic his wife was playing away.
I worried for him—suffered all she might

be wanting, all the shaming why,
taxis and bewildered pavements, strange
landscapes lasting an hour

and living for them I began to change
shrivelling in the hands of my own Power
channelling the stress out of them into me

until they parted painlessly
and Stevie told the press
her secret changed in my fantasy,

how, lacking any, I had stole his stress
as though I'd worn his suit, her frock.

Then I was laughed at as a holy freak
but hired to worry for a billionaire,
divert his enervating ifs,

living the self he needed to ignore,
joining his nurses, minders, low-fat chefs.
I looked down dizzy from the peak of his rise

alarmed by his empire of sweets and cakes—
as though his body stretched its boundaries
I felt inside him how such bigness aches

that what was one is now so many,
speaking for him, acting his role.
All this was changeable as money,
edging always out of control.

When he was shot, instead of spare
parts I gave my whole self like a martyr:
we breathed together in intensive care,
wounds flowering in me like stigmata.

All the media wanted their share
and hundreds started to suffer
pain so big no body could contain
that burst from him and fell like rain
and when we started to recover
all proclaimed a miracle:
I hired the scapegoats who together
struck themselves down with the bleeding call.

My surrogates: each like a mother
lends their body to another

paying ourselves like a price
wearing like coins another's face
finding problems not our own

running on our skin like lice,
hearing in silence as though down the phone
blanketed by noise a slight cry

demanding our sacrifice

burning our skin as though the sun shone
solely on us through the hole in the sky

I'm English, and wicked

I'm English in this Hollywood thriller
and it's not that I'm a killer
shocks you but the tilt of my jaw,
my snooty vowels and elegant suit,
this air that one was born above the law.
The crime I plotted in my Tuscan villa

involves a labyrinth of wire,
a map of the sewers and a worried timer.
I hold New York to complex ransom
while looking obnoxiously handsome
and torturing a social climber.
Centuries now, in a green shire,

my family's been the land it sat on,
and ships that carried cotton, slaves and tea.
The halflit alleyways of history
echo and twist and lead to me.
But what went wrong was Eton,
perhaps, where I was buggered and beaten

so I'm not, you see, quite fully male.
My voice is pitched a little high
and that is why I'm bound to fail,
my bomb can't blow the big reactor.
Look at the shoulders on the good guy
who mumbles like a method actor,

this stubbly American pachyderm.
He won't be shaken from my trail.
He's driven. I'm the stubborn frontier
he'll push at like a pioneer
smelling of buffalo, leather and sperm,
the white symbolic whale

he's hot for and relies on
to put him to the troubling test
that stops him thinking and makes him act—
pretending one could push forever west
stirred up like a face some woman's smacked,
and wanting to stand on the watery horizon.

The Adman's Breakdown

My mind was deep in shoes
that 5 a.m. my dad had died.
I'd worked on how in shoes the tongue
is tied down tight: it could unloose
and speak —but now that went all wrong.
The shoes had let me down. They lied.

I grew up watching my dad's
ideas he'd talked about —between
my programs, clever, funny ads
where jolly brave homunculi
were fighting the kitchen clean.
He made the products hear and see

and entered their needy spirit,
their needing to be needed
that powered their sexy allure.
The teasing prospects that inspire it
made me say, one day, he traded
only tricks, he was a liar —

but after I grew excited
by what an ad-man can command:
I saw the screen grow sensitive
as though responding to my hand,
I felt my own desire requited
watching the products change, and live:

this sofa longs to feel
a body enter its embrace;
this car's familiar with a place
where mountains melt into an ocean,
clouds at dawn are parting to reveal
frustrations dispersing in constant motion —

until that 5 a.m.
when shoes were sticking out their tongues.
The things —I grew so scared of them,
their quiet voices, hidden thought.
Hoovers were humming manic songs.
And all the things dad bought,

I never believed as much in —
these appliances that learn to talk,
conspiring in the dark of the kitchen,
televisions that learn to walk:
the screen's big brain that springs to life
a fork that whispers, a smiling knife.

Boggart Holes

His parents whispered in the next room—
straining to hear was like this long
attempting to realise.
Numb shadows in the fog like constables
poke canes into the frosted tufts,
flowing smoothly as a punting flotilla
but raising the tips to their noses.
A deep perforation was widening
under his bed. He feared the falling backwards
into a darkness whose surface
the constables stir, from which the outcrops heaved
that experts dust for fossil prints.

He fears the darkness sifting underfoot
from holes, the boggart mouths,
their faces lined in staring eiderdown:
to be as lost as the armchair and the couch,
a lounge leaking foam into this rainy col,
eroding with their knowledge into waste.
So warned, his reconstructions are their motives
as identikits are faces;
as lights begin to simplify the valley,
delineate a town by numbers,
he animates the murderers, that pair,
like Mickie and Minnie slowed to jerking stills.

How Does It Feel?

Lines On Tony Harrison's Gulf War poems

He saw the photo on the Sunday,
started writing on the Monday

how the dead Iraqi spoke
like Palinurus or that bloke

in 'Strange Meeting': you'll have read
before about the talking dead—

no problem then for this charred head,
except for how and what it said,

for when it leant into his mike
it sounded like a pissed-off tyke,

it sounded like his loiner dad,
someone a world away from Bagdad,

his windscreen wiper like a biro
he's reaching for to sign a giro.

It seemed obsessed with sperm banking
and accused the yanks of wanking—

though spilling sperm's a minor guilt,
compared to all the blood they spilt

and this was just a metaphor
of the poet's you'll have read before:

The Waste Land and D.H.Lawrence
express symbolic abhorrence—

linking fruitless sexual practices
with decadence and cactuses;

they say we can't now ripen our oats
(this isn't literal—see the 'Notes').

But notions so Weston sound all wrong
from that burned and foreign tongue,

whose last thoughts surely were a far cry
likewise from 'epiphany'—

that writer reaching for his pen,
the cold coming and the three wise men.

And if you interview a charred head
 ('How does it feel, then, being dead?')

let him speak in his own voice,
not like a Yorkshireman or James Joyce.

That photograph and its violence
sit in an alien silence

where a fraught polyphony
might speak, but not epiphany—

transcendant insights that replace
missed moments of religious grace

are not just missing but unmissed
as a quill in a cindery fist

in that least meaningful of wars
made cosier by these metaphors.

Dead Eliot, Lawrence and James Joyce
could characterise a voice,

suggesting a sound reflective
of another's distinct perspective—

this was what was needed to suggest
the gulf between that head and the West:

how sounds happened in him—speech and song,
the foreign landscape of his tongue.

Parys Mountain 1

It was a lesson for my youth; sublime
in Burke's sense of terror enjoyed:
a scene John Martin might have painted
who combines Milton and mines.
For hell was everywhere underfoot.

Lowered into the gulf the poor souls
were weighed in corves; infernal heat
rising, and the spilt veins, inflamed the marl.
And later, when disused—its sulphur and ghosts,
its fiery pitfalls under heather!

Too old for fell-walking I enjoy, now,
that soul-testing exercise across
an inward, torturous terrain.
The lake I lie on mingles umber and shades
burning with sunset and reflected copper.

On its surface I stretch my fingers
like a pauper's over cracks where mud
oozes through his cellar floor.
This is the great gulf inverted, with its souls
anatomised like Burked bodies—a glove,

emptied, pressing coins into a fob; a shoe,
disembodied, poised for blacking.
But the rocks that rain on me are nothing like
the crumbs I wouldn't share
that tumbled from my table.

Parys Mountain 2

What worried us about the old workings
drew our kids who always returned
with war-painted knees. We set out now
in a red light, thinking of feathers
scattered along a sulphurous adit.

Cowboys and indians are staining the West.
A gorse bush bulges from a van frame
gagging its jaw-like hood: we strive towards
childhood and find the afterlife of ovens
and fridges, skeletal metals, badlands.

Slowly in the fire of pigments a rug
is being consumed to sparse sutures—
so we tread softly, treading
on nightmares and enjoying it like
our houses on fire, thinking of our wives

and our red hands and alert to smoke signals
feet might raise in the coppery dust, and ancient
childish voices that ascend the dark shafts.
The flayed open-cast reminds us of
wincing from touch. Our reasons for being here

are changing, or we enter a vacant place
between reasons, and although turning back
we meet our children half-way, we emerge
bunched for comfort like cars from fog,
in line and shining their cautious lights.

Phallic Shit

The damp of my mother's bed, the damp warm,
and the trail across her sheets

of her month-long lovers, summon
this slowest swarm

pushed out from the wet hill
through the cracks in our back door

to stretch out on the walls like an omen
in the morning in our kitchen.

I touch one
curled across the light switch,

one sizzles on a ring as it heats,
one cringes from my finger-nail

pushed into the tip of a rubber glove.
The kitchen feels them like an itch,

so featureless they're not a creature
but a blunt ooze

verging on nothing or water
and raw as a weeping sore,

each one a loose end
looking for something to love.

I salt them and they turn to semen,
but I'm guilty and identify

and think of secret pleasures
where my self dissolves,

and how they lose themselves
and blend

into nothing or nature,

how they're scared of salt the way a butterfly
is scared of scissors.

Freeze Frame

A household is threatened by forces that could open it up.
    A tannoy echoed in the living-room
Of a couple I knew whose house looked down on trains and platforms.
    It unnerved me like a homely showroom,
Warm light on armchairs, serried lounges, all in a windy field.
    Perhaps the pressures rose then forced a change.
Lamplight had shone behind the curtains which embayed it like
    Their intimacy and the walls, but then
Maybe it had started to feel provisional—
    A shelter somehow not complete; rising,
Destinations prised a way through the furniture.
    Through a door left open I stumble
Detective-like into a frame isolated from a plot.
    On the table is a disappointed lead
Coiled towards its kettle, and leaves where he must have split
    The coupled tea bags. One of them had said
You're walling me in, for through a quarter circle
    Back and forward an erect umbrella rocks
On its pins, and I can hear two strangers in the bathroom—
    Conversation drifted there in the wind.
What ought to be inward was prised open, until they were
    Cohabiting with North Atlantic moods.
Their thoughts linger head-high above the pine-table, tangled
    As the flight-paths of a cloud of midges.
A cold front has spread from the kitchen. Causes tangle
    With symptoms; onions nude in vinegar
Jarred and smarting shudder on their old refrigerator
    That palpitates and wheezes, pumping its breath
Into a flat frozen in the puzzled look of a photograph
    Its subjects have vacated. Two stiffs
Are clasped together in the teapot like a couple in lava.
    Leavers and arrivers are embarrassed:
High above the platform the lit casement is uncurtained,
    Exposing its hurt interior to the dark.

A Coypu

Lovers between them can make
another mind whose ideas
neither apart would conceive
resembling folie a deux
as wishes resemble fears.

Lovers together even see
differently from each apart,
or so I thought after that walk
between the fenced-in marsh and the shore:
that creature hurried from you and me

down a line we wrote together—
neither of us could be sole author
both of its strong claws and its webbed feet.
Interacting we assembled
this tubby, furry other

pulling a tail like an afterthought.
I started as though from the danger
of what we'd make of one another
if my wishes conspired with yours.
The couple we are is a stranger

like the bright owl we must've made up
ghosting from the trees into a brief
tiff with a crow, then off through the park
a thousand miles south of its range
like stories we invent jointly that return
as memories, and haunt belief.

The Great Escape

After school he'll visit his grandfather
Who used to be a prisoner of war.
The people move so freely outside the home—
With wincing care, inside, and slow Zimmer frames.

Surely this can't hold his grandfather:
He'll escape his neighbour who complains
Someone's been digging her grave all night,
That her bifocals throw the ground into her eyes.

A prisoner of war like his grandfather
Can dig his way into the youthful streets.
So near he's come but his abandoned tunnels
Veered into sewers and electric cables:

Once you're under, sighs his grandfather,—
Ask the dead—it's hard to climb back up:
Often they find a gutter guarded by bars.
But always he finds his friends down there, his wife,

Mother and father, grandmothers and grandfathers,
And the colours of the waiting Spring.
He's looking forward to the past
His dig unearths like storeys under the floor:

The soil reaches out towards his grandfather,
Heaps of darkness growing under his bed,
The soil in daylight weights his holed pockets
But sprinkles from him, lightening his burden,

Preparing the release of his grandfather—
Downwards and then up. Out of biology
The escaping grandson gallops, frowning
At sunlight, clutching a sparkling Easter egg.

The Breakwater

Her drowned fingers brushed the breakwater —
This haunted the surveyor checking for damp:
He knew for all his fifty years the old woman
Who lived before her strange death in this house.
Widowed, she closed the seaview bedroom's door,
'For ever'. As a child he passed the room,
Watching the sea swarm across its window,

Breaking across the shadowy bed.
Where wife and husband used to sleep
Was an absence like the nothing up a sleeve
Hanging flatly from a jacket.
Imagine a young couple in the bedroom
She abandoned to the sea noises, where she drowned
All their past! This haunted the surveyor:

She must have confused her husband with the sea —
Its brief identities shuffled together,
And vanishing. The room must have wavered in the bay,
A slow dissolve that read: Fifty Years Before.
The sea must have started where the landing ended
Though the house still felt the room
Like the ache in a severed arm.

Dream's boundaries vary like the tide,
Waking shores itself with crumbling walls.
She must have thought her husband had come back
When the waves cast their past on the landing
And she slipped into a sleep like an undertow,
Entering the surprising extension
With its snoring shingle and its drowned wall.

in the twin city

here are word pictures
they will help me learn the nice language
of the twin city

in the twin city
you are small and blonde but you are still you

in the stuffed subway the loathed bodies
also there I
grieve that you are lost

by the glass buildings the feared hollow
through the lost centre the desired buses

in the twin language
there are seven words which I can make
the required sentence

your surprised double
offers me a new beginning

near the warm harbour the entwined railways

I am sober or mislay the keys
to the red escort
take a safe taxi back that lost Friday

all the massed raindrops on the bright railings
hold the ghost centre but will break

by the glass buildings the repeat action
where I take my second chance
do not meet by chance that same Friday
your farouche sister

near the brick arches by the past river
mirrored by the massed windows

in the nice bedsit near the ghost harbour
on the same duvet
look it is beginning to recur

how the far mountains
are like hope and glassed
in the past river

through the glassed centre
number seven buses drive and do not stop
but will go on through the north suburbs
searching searching

Animations

      I'd hardly thought of you at all
recently—it'd been so long, and how and where we lived
      differed so much. There'd been your call
it must be five years ago, you'd met by chance (and this revived
      a distance between us from when
we'd been close) an old girlfriend of mine, and I'd decided
      when we spoke again
I'd try to explain what happened, which was more than one-sided:
      but how could you see, being gay,
David, what I'd seen in her? Even with friends there's a gulf
      between us and the foreign way
they live—your business animation, and producing
      Rolf Harris'Cartoon Time, you'd fly
to eastern Europe and America to buy cartoons—
      but what you did would pass me by
like half a sentence heard by a driver as he tunes
      his radio and deciphers a sign,
except his destination and the broken clause
      mingle and so redefine
themselves and him, if slightly. So my life is swayed by yours
      as though by air apparently
still, yet infiltrating because in our formative years
      the gulf between you and me
was part of how I saw the adulthood we entered,
      silence, failure of affinity:
learning how for each the world is questionably centred.
      Now I'm husband, father of two
and the tadpoles are a virus under a microscope
      wriggling their tails, when I review
that day with Sue away: I cook, play, self-consciously cope,
      for the day in question changes
in the light of that evening, when a casual reference
      on television rearranges
March 21st from your perspective, and its severance.

       Quick shifts in points of view disrupt
expectations: upshots, downshots Chuck Jones used in *Bugs Bunny*—
       you enthused...Life's also abrupt,
I said: its camera shifts, its witty and unfunny
       angles show us up. And thought
how stills, spliced and multiplied, resemble movement as stories
       life, though slices, added up, distort
the felt continuities of self. My '80's worries
       were a caricature: you'd bought
a flat together, you and Ian, and must know the risks
       better than a straight like me, you two
metropolitan, street-smart, invulnerable as compact discs.

       I lived with my family and my view
of the mountains and the Menai Straits, and sometimes missed you
       recalling the naked rugby scrum
you fantasised about in Physics, or the fireman who kissed you
       in *Napoleon's*, but the sum
of all these slices won't add up to life: upstairs on a bus
       once, I said I wouldn't want to be
a father, and you said you would, some day you would. How does
       it happen? We, my children and me
set out to search for pondweed, worrying for our tadpoles
       without it; Paul stops for a pee
and wets his socks; we watch the lambs; I don't compare our roles,
       your tasteful, toy-uncluttered flat,
my semi: keep my temper, cook a pizza, kiss them better;
       Sue is back, it's 7 and we're sat
half-watching T.V. and I say I've taught Paul a letter,
       pressing *Play*, half-thinking that
Tracey Macleod is tremblingly beautiful, for I've recorded
       Late Again, and watch her eyes
follow her cue, which says Chuck Jones has been awarded
       the first David Platt memorial prize.

Why I'm Too Cowardly to Have a Vasectomy

Because I think I ought to understand what my *vas* is before they cut it out.

Because I had a cyst cut out once from my lower lip and the nurse couldn't find the right scalpel

And the doctor said *You'd better go and look for it then* and settled back to wait

Except he had already cut the lip open and had to hold it shut

And I lay back looking at a strip-light and he described the path he was making in his garden, how he'd had to kill the weeds, then dig and dig and tamp and tamp then spread the gravel

And I replied with my eyebrows and tight noises in my throat

Imagining the nurse walking intricatecorridorsandclimbing endless stairs, searching cupboards with infinite compartments

And she came back empty-handed and the doctor squeezed my lip tighter and said *We'll talk about this later— I'll have to use this*

And I never saw what 'this' was.

It's not because I think my life depends on my *vas*, or depends *from* it—

I've never been promiscuous and I've never been much good at fighting or drinking:

But we men are so confused now—we wouldn't know our *vas* from our elbow;

Because I think I ought to understand what my *vas* is before they cut it out.

It's because I want to think of something secluded in me waiting for when I might need it, or not

And because I see my legs hoisted up gynaecologically—and think of what they do to women!—

And the doctor riffles deftly through his cutlery tray, and says
Oh well, I'll have to use <u>this</u>.

Deconstructionists on Fast Forward

On Channel 4 the pundits find it
Terribly hard not drowning
But signing on the waves

Rippling across the screen;
They frisk an absent body,
Meaning slips through their fingers

Like bubbles from their mouths:
Faced with the failure of words
The deconstructionists

Throw up their hands
As though desiring words made flesh,
The dove descending—

Or a fantasy of the deaf
Seeing what they mean,
Bodies in the shape of a word:

Deft hands astonish deaf faces
And from their sleeves ideas
Emerge, unfolding their wings.

Shadowing

Who my employers are I've never known,
Nor what they have in mind for Marcus Ring.
The woman was persuasive on the phone,
Since then it's been all watching, shadowing—
We two like distant partners in a dance.
I've studied all the cuttings I was sent
Until his memories rise in me like my own:
Schooldays, Cambridge, marriage, high finance,
Then politics, the rise in Parliament.

I've watched him with his daughter and her soft toys
Sprawled on the carpet; also with a slow pen
Glinting towards me from his anglepoise;
And calming a farmer in a cold fen.
I've loitered, noting the particulars
Of meetings of the party, or committees—
Never with Russians, gangsters, hired girls or boys;
My forearms aching from binoculars,
I've watched his innocence in five cities.

Unless my stranger's vision is selective,
Making patterns in advance, forcing rhymes
With what's expected by a tired detective,
Partial because excluded, blind to crimes
Flagrant to insiders. If my own
Routine were watched, how would it look?
My neck stiffens with the strange perspective
Watching my back—the woman, say, on the phone.
My actions mistranslated in a notebook.

Snuffed candles, bitten apple, smiling face—
Mere freaks of my attention linger,
Impasses, not clues to his disgrace.
That farmer bridles; where he points his finger
Broadens and dissolves into the coming night:
I'm tired of the vain hope for scandal,
My sense of purpose bewildered in such space.
His wife, one evening, switches off the light
And then is lighting candle after candle,

And they close their eyes, I think—I strain to see.
They fall on all fours. He crawls around the couch,
She frisks the walls. Is this a parody
Of my blindness—how they move by touch?
I shrink into my shell as they collide
Hair, mouths and throats, and vanish in a grapple.
Later, near Ely, I hunker in a tree,
Darkly, in his garden, envying his side—
His daughter's playmate drops a bitten apple,

Boy and girl both naked.But how far from grace
I've fallen, and from who I used to be!
The mirror shocks me with my own face,
Now it belongs to someone not quite me
Whose wife and daughter left him from neglect,
Who follows on a lead—who has no choice,
Whose world is nothing but the case.
I've followed Ring so long that I affect
His pensive gestures, languid posture, stage voice:

I think it's me sometimes in committee—
I deploy all the details, they're impressed,
I'm going to transform the inner city.
Then they're shocked: I'm wearing just an oil-streaked vest,
I falter, digress—my breached defences
Threaten theirs ... Yet powerful hands, in secret, tie
We two into a fraught complicity:
He glanced up right into my lenses
Once, and smiled, as though I were his alibi,

As though he likes to lead me in a dance,
Courting this private (like the public) eye,
Forcing on me strict patterns in advance,
Knowing that I've grown to need them, to rely
Even on the sad hope for scandals,
That I fear most feeling lost, as when that fen
Bewildered the thin spoor with distance:
Bright narcissi in a breeze, like candles,
Guttered and left me in the dark again.

I need imposed on me a cramped space
Of self—strong hands to lead my steps, a set
Course, the will of others, and to know my place:
My course would open like a road-map, that net
Of choices, and devour me if I were dismissed,
Or scatter me into nothing and nowhere—
A cringing blur out of my carapace,
Or taut balloon drifting from a tight first,
A tiny stretch at risk from too much air.

Thomas the Tank Engine Reaches Puberty

Thomas thought he was a train—
Pistoned his arms and chanted *choo-choo,*
Gathered speed and said as he ran
I think I am I think I am I think I am

He woke out of a restless dream
And found his blood was steam
His face a silver disc
His voice the many wheels
That said as they ran
I think I am I think I am I think I am

Could he be an engine?
All his friends boy-engines too?
No mummies and
No daddies and
No teachers?
All day chanting *choo-choo-choo*?
Wanted to stop this thinking
And to say as he ran
I think I am I think I am I think I am

Then he noticed girls
Who had wheels and windows
Corridors and comfy seats
Were helpless carriages,
Were lacking steam and pistons,
Needed Thomas or another engine—
Needed marriages—
Even to say as they ran
I think I am I think I am I think I am

But then he noticed also
All the world was a shallow sham—
The country where the rails ran
A mere facade for miles and miles,
Merely puppets all the people—
Stiff their postures, forced their smiles.
Surely Thomas must be real—
His wheels worried as they ran:
I think I am I think I am I think I am

He grew and grew and grew
Obsessed with tunnels and with couplings—
And his steam sang *choo-choo-choo*
And his steam surged inside him
And he charged along the track,
Hurtled off the rails
And landed on his back.
The moon looked down on a silver disc
Frowning like a boy's face,
Glinted on the slowing wheels
That could no longer
Say as they ran
I think I am I think I am I think I am

Thomas was sick for weeks and weeks
Being mended in the works
And when he was as good as new
Worried he was not the same choo-choo
Because he had such different parts:
Said, 'Am I Thomas now or who?
I'm Thomas and not you or you'
And his new wheels said as they ran
I think I am I think I am I think I am

The Hawk at the Shrink

Imagine, said his analyst,
A salt marsh.

Behind his shut lids
The darkness persisted,
And persisted.

Then he saw an old wall,
Weathered from without
And eaten from within;
Unyielding, standing up
Against the salt wind.
For long service, this wall's
Decorated with lichens.

No, his analyst said,
Imagine a salt marsh.

The land he can grasp,
The sea imagine.
But their mingling—
Like water and air,
A grey day—
The frosty weather he prefers,
Its hard clear light
Affirms each object—
Separate, itself.

His analyst was firm.
She said: *Together,*
Sea and land.

There followed an expensive silence.

Then, dismayed:
Receded tide,
Slovenly foreshore;
Slack meander where
The spineless river
Loses itself.
Small heaps of
Soft phalluses,
A thousand bubbles
Bursting under mud—
Shrill murmur of
Feminine victory

The land and water
He mistrusts; but he admires
Fire, which is itself,
Or nothing.

Voice Over

Your closest ally in your government
Leans on two surprised words till they dissent
From themselves, and stumble into menace.
Others conspire to threaten sentences.
Doubt loiters with Intent, Defy with Die:
You fly, drive and drive and hole up in Venice.

You'd feel at home in the quattrocento,
You're not a tourist puzzling this memento
Of fear and glory, needing to ignore one
To feel the other—brilliant propaganda,
Stolen saint and bronze horses and thunder,—
Falling between two minds in oxymoron.

The Doge's Palace has division in-built,
Contrary chambers, wide and narrow; secret guilt:
Inside the sculptured head of this lion
The throat's a box for delations; a tiny keyhole
Turns this wall into a door, which turns
Gilt and marble into stone and iron.

You think of the arsenal and the ghetto
As you walk recesses Tintoretto
Has not endorsed with triumph or allegory:
Those legacies and this—to be removed
Down corridors, across a bridge, past a hateful
Glimpse of San Giorgio Maggiore.

A tiny key can turn inside a word,
Reversing all to which it had referred,
Startling at its back the resonance
Of bare chambers, echoing stone stairs,
And oubliettes of voices in your country.
Fear made Venice threaten, pray and think askance—

It built a castle to defend its wealth,
Churches to petition God for health—
On threatened foundations, wary premises—
Feared Hell, high water and Black Death; but throve:
So made this Palace from the castle;
Suffered, though not that last nemesis

Of flood and plague. But in a state of fear
Some words dissemble, others disappear
And leave you acting out a baffled mime
Voiced over in a language not your own.
Ghost-written others echo at the mikes;
Encode and hint, divide or quietly rhyme.

Fast Asleep

The driver fell asleep at the wheel
as though the edge where she'd been pushed
crumbled and she fell, but floated
and the car continued regardless
with its windscreen like a TV
turbid with disputing heads—
the merger had pushed her to the edge
and they were shouting it was wrong, wrong!—
her cigarette was burning
fifty seconds from her fingers
but her wheels were inching to the left
as the motorway was sloping
under the light rain and flashes of sun
down towards the sunlit city
where the river broadened,
all before her shut eyes
so when she looked into the windscreen
she saw her husband smile and
whisper in that woman's ear
as she careered below a kestrel
that dipped, then rose, then hovered
like a moment of stuck time

Fast Asleep Too

The driver fell asleep at the wheel:
his colleagues always admired
the way, with setbacks, he could
continue regardless—not knowing
he was knotted hard like a golfer
locked up tight into his backswing
and forbidden to unwind—
but now his hands softened, and his head
slackened—just in the middle
of everything, the long dispute
with his father, and the lack
of closure with his wife—
his wipers can't erase
these pictures in his windscreen,
and he's a thread pulling loose
in the middle of the network—
direction signs that stare at him,
the slip road not taken,
and the haven of the service station,
headlights in his mirrors
igniting through the rain—
but the middle lane's like home to him
and shelters him for miles:
as though he could continue asleep
into the city and his parking-space,
sleepwalk into the purposeful lobby,
then hum in the lift to the fifteenth floor,
and his screen that welcomes him by name.

Elusive Boy

It's mum. That's posh now, this machine—
It's like you though, you were always clever:
'I'm out right now, but speak after the tone.'
But what I wanted was to thank you, Dean,
For the car, and also Trevor
Wants to thank you, but won't phone.
We've washed the tyres and hid the spade and fork—

We love the car, don't get me wrong,
Though Trevor says it's been through hell.
He's saying you and him should talk—
That 'model' and that queer, you don't belong
With them. But Dean, please, give me a bell.

It's Jane. I've been to the flat four times.
You didn't say you were going.
Like a fool I tidied the place up.
I know about your little crimes,
Remember—your toing and froing
And wheeling and dealing.
                              Face up
To us—apart from me there's no-one
To care about the Dean you bury
Under all that con and pose.
Your friends have nothing to go on.

Why leave in such a hurry
You scatter the floor with clothes
As though the real you and your disguises
Are tangled in a fight?...

It always stirs me, mind, imagining
Several of you (though in the same sizes)
Helping me make it through the night.
Soon as you get back, give me a ring.

Jeff here... Who's an elusive boy?
You're badly missed by my better half
Who made up my mind to phone you.
Why did you get so troubled and coy?

You're more than just a member of staff,
And ever since we've known you,
You've used yourself, you were your own ploy
And dressed up for a laugh,
And no-one said we own you,
So why should you disappear?
Unless to 'find yourself'
(Though what you find won't be you at all).
Unless it was out of fear
Of how you've redefined yourself.
Come back soon and give us a call.

It's Trevor. Oh, you'd be in stitches—
But I do feel your thoughts, your mindset—
Though you'd listen to your own twin
Less than those telephone bitches
Rubbing their clothes against the handset.
Open your lines, please. Let me tune in.

It's Jane. Don't leave me this way.
I ought to kick you. Once I fought a
War to get clean, then felt I'd fallen
Flat into a straight day.

The world has turned to water,
I'm a teabag leaking and all swollen.
Once I reached my hand out in the night
And touched, not you, but the edge of a trench
Which crumbled. It was for a drain.
The steps led down a flight,
But there were clothes rotting. And the stench!
Come back. I get no kick from cocaine.

It's Trevor. Somehow you're gone now
More than before, when I have flowed
Out blindly to reach you along
The streets of thought. I'm down to one now
And need to speak to lift this load
Off my chest, and the crumbs of soil of my tongue.

Jeff here. Call if you're around, I'm worried.
You're lost wherever you are—
You'll be wearing the colours of that place.
How many of you have you buried?
After we'd pushed through a crowd, once, you wore
Somebody else's face.

You've grown up to be multi-storied
But I still think of the boy you were,
A glue-sniffing naif and hard case,
Dying to be someone, and becoming
Three initials on a Jag's plates,
Endless changes of clothes,
And now this dumb phone—you're all-consuming...

Like a fire underground that depletes
Itself, and hollows out the more it grows.

It's me. I don't know why you went.
Now I have to talk to this hissing
Of distance, this hissing of no-one there:
Though talk was a dead letter sent
To you always, to somebody missing,
Or never how they seem, pointless as prayer.

Carriers of the End

'... I mean such as had received the contagion, and had it really upon them, and in thir blood, yet did not show the consequences... These were the dangerous people;'
                              Daniel Defoe, A Journal of the Plague Year

'Once, when a whore accosted me, I bowed, 'I deeply regret it, Madam, but I have a friend.' Once I carved on a seat in the park. 'We have sat here. You'd better not...'.'
                              W.H. Auden, Letter to a Wound

The enemy Defoe identified
Were limpers, wore white caps and scarves tied
Around their necks; the looks of others lied,
Resembled ours four hours before they died.

They've stood in moonlit forests side by side—
The pastor and polluted wretches-cried
To the devil, watched the witches ride
On the air. In daylight they subvert us undescried.

They saucered here because their planet died.
They hate our values but they hide
In human form, except they're laser-eyed,
Their feet are webbed. They're plants inside.

They're really reptiles but they've occupied
Your boss, your daughter—live because they died.

They've chronic wounds they've closeted inside
Their normal clothes; in letters they confide:
'I love you, wound. Please be my bride.'

The wounds are quiet, or they've lied,
And spawned in other hosts, and multiplied.

Following the Charts

The secrets of the X-ray and the tests his wife
Wouldn't guess, he seemed the same, and he confided
only with his boat, which looked at him askance.
His wife was jealous of *Rebecca*, said it widowed her —
and often that unsettled autumn he slept below her deck
preferring to his wife the boatyard's sisterhood,
their naked halyards screaming in the wind, stuck fast
like an envelope in a blustery hedge.
He caulked *Rebecca*'s wooden splits and fissures,
healed her paintwork: dying is easier like this,
turned into a destination to arrive at,
stocking up the fridge, remembering the flares
and life jackets that make him suddenly smile.
He carries around the doctor's forecast
like cargo in his hold, together with a colour
like tiger lilies, the hinted lure of what is far off
trapped amongst the boatyard's ragwort, and uncanny growth,
knowledge he should've happened on before

this morning in Spring: the hoisted sails, *Rebecca*
looking at him askance again because he thinks
that she's the answer, and this late beginning where water
swells and deepens — but the currents are charted — and the heat builds.

The Creature from the Black Lagoon (U.S. 1952)

       Monsters are attracted to women—
I mean those 50s man-made figments in films.
       The men can't understand the woman,
The lagoon, the gentle monster, because they're like
       Water-skiers skimming the deep's surface
Elegantly; when the webbed, hairy claw is thrust
       Into the port-hole they recognise it
Like someone alone with flu discovering
       The distances, the bad climate
In his house—their premises grow strange as though
       A river were running under them.

The gillman is half man, half fish and half fear, half wish;
       The woman, in her 50s way,
Invites him—she's always undressing, always
       Standing to one side of the group
Flirting with the night, like children in a tent
       Sleeping in the garden, who want
The front door left ajar. So, now, their threshold darkens:
       The leading man is dozing,
The woman is changing her clothes again, the gillman
       Rises from his spacious ulterior—
But only to have a look. The men are business men,
       Though, and scientists; these frogmen must
Follow the monster under the water and above
       Into its dripping labyrinth—
They've come to catch a wish for their aquarium.
       Instead they find they've poisoned the fish,
Which lie limp on the surface looking sideways at them.
       Their confidence is shaken, like that
Of a water-skier glimpsing all he's standing on;
       They've angered the monster, they must escape.
A grasping desire has exiled them from the lagoon
       Making them feel in their own element
Like fish out of water. And when the film ends, I'm like
       A frogman waiting to rise,
Treading water just below the surface, learning
       To breathe again at a lower pressure.

Vengeance is Mine

The two were perfect friends,
Except they judged each other
Harshly over tidiness.
Only death would part them—
One was Catholic,
The other Anglican.

Sooner than they thought
They parted: from her window
The Anglican watches
Trying to imagine
What Hell means to her friend, this Hell
Lying about her in her old age.

Since tidiness obsesses her
She must employ her walking-stick,
Eternally, to clear leaves
And litter from the street
Which grows fraught with meaning
Like a poem by God:

Its wicked never rest.
Its proud continually fall.
The author of her suffering
Shakes the autumn through downpours
At her hesitating feet;
The leaves are carried like lost souls
Forward and back in the wind.

Whose vengeance is this?

Sighs and lamentations
Swell from the railway-line,
The next circle; for the souls
Shrieking in the playground
Third childhoods last the longest—
Spinning and swinging
And jerking up and down.

Poor dear, she peers up
Through her thick glasses
And can't remember where she is.

The Vicar and the Rag and Bone Man

He looks and beholds a pale horse
trotting past the consecrated ground
that rises from his half-demolished parish.

Brick dust and splinters fly in the faces
of four angels—air and vacancy
church light irradiates into form—

who, higher than the half-completed flats,
survey interiors wet with rain,
staircases climbing to the open.

At corners the rag and bone man rides
into vacated feelings, and reoccupies them.
Legs and arms tangle on his cart.

His rags remember bones, shaped to their contours;
crumbs of skin cling to their clothes; a mirror,
broken, hatches dead faces in glass.

The angels sound their trumpets
above these revelations,
and predatory hearses circle the estate.

Happy the Man

A general in my pensive retreat,
Self-exiled from all parties and sects,
In my own ground I wrought the sacred cause
Higher into the gardener's effects.

And so God's seasons, like my moods,
Were glassed in all that we had made
Until the lichens started, suddenly,
Shrivelling on the colonnade.

The glass held only me—until I was,
Not banished from the garden, but joined there:
Benches on my seat, and thoughts of others
Rippling my standing pool of air.

Glittering in the chandeliers, hazy
In the billiard room's southward view,
Manchester was looming, more substantial
Than my scagliola and ormolu.

The terrace flickered with interference,
With man-made fibres walking mongrels, ghosts
Washed up from a council estate, from air
Stirred into waves by wires and masts

—Which lifted reflections from those waves
And lined the clouds, showering traces
Not of God, across the park, but voices,
And a snow of faces melting on the leaves.

A Dislocation

When I was five and my father died
I started to stutter.

Where we lived when I was five
is difficult—

a stretch of carpet leading to a door.
It struggles just to *be* a place,

no ceiling and no walls,
no storeys above or underneath

like words that shut themselves tight
away from me—

no sister and no baby brother,
floral carpet hovering and fading,

and my mother off to one side,
and hardly even me

who's five now,
where words are difficult to climb.

The Sick Room

A man reading *The Daily Herald*,
a woman and her pram, struggling with a bag,
a girl skipping and talking to her doll,
two workmen running in overalls—
my father jerked his hand up pushing them away
as they passed through the curtains and door over his bed.
I was five. My mother wouldn't let me see how hard
the room was taking it. It wasted away,
worn to nothing by pedestrians filing through.
Colour was draining from the roses on the wall.
The ceiling thinned, letting in the sky.
Tarmac was emerging through the floor.
My father whitened, turning into his sheets.
One morning there were street noises behind the door.
The city repossessed the room, swept the curtains back.
Distances entered. Last time I went there,
the room had been worn to a pavement by the feet.

A Dental Appointment

The old kitchen, just before:
her arms heaped with washing, mouth gagged with pegs.
The walls sloughed and grew two skins,
cupboards fattened, smelling of paint,
the table lengthened and shone.

I'd hurried home, was missing my appointment,
while she was lying on the couch.
Twelve neighbours were pronouncing,
superstitiously, upon the danger,
when combined, of washing-day and dentistry.

My jagged tooth had done it.
Her right side was softening
into a mist I parted: the arm
was deadened, and the leg calipred.
And all the peggies on the carpet!

The couch was growing into the suite
it would be after she returned.
Her mouth fell open: all her conversations
chattered out high-pitched, rewinding;
her sentences were scrambled after.

Ambulance men removed the old furniture,
the pegs were broken on the stone floor.
My tongue tested the half-gap of the snag,
my roots aching over older incisors;
removal men stretchered her away.

Her Mother's Way

And while my mother was away
her mother came and took control,
and after felt she had to stay
as though my mother must replay
all of her childhood trying to be whole.

My mother now was *Jean*.
Our house was altered to her mother's way,
her loud stilettos and her knitting machine,
the pullover that chatters and unfurls,
the secret pocket sweetened with eclairs,
the miniature poodle and the soft grey curls,
the wool-balls jumping where she sat.

And then my mother never dares
to sit around with friends and smoke
but being again her mother's daughter
must be punished for her stroke
and learn again to walk and talk
watched by the woman who first taught her.

And my mother lived twelve years like that.

From Whose Bourn

My mother had a stroke, and you,
Her mother, came to take her place—
Continued when she died.

This wintry photo of you
And the beach at Newborough Warren
That day in summer, they're combined now:

For in the photo your hand
Shades your cataracts as though
Peering after me a beach away.

That day the summer was uncertain
Like a memory; I walked
Miles to find the sea, and you,

Behind me, were a wave growing smaller.
Two yachts, the shore apart,
Placed the sea between quotation marks.

I drove to Newborough again today—
A day in winter uncertain
Like a memory, as though

Two pages had turned forward at once
Into summer, or as though summer's
Writing showed through under winter's:

A flock of birds like a heat-haze
On the flickering horizon, a cloud of midges,
Bright deceptive sun and warmth like a reprieve

Except for the ice
Stretching the shore's length in a frozen bourn
Wide as a single-track road,

The warm spell suggesting a return
Except for the ice-road,
The one-way traffic of the dead.

A year ago I raised my voice—
Poor hearing made you seem far off.
And through the camera lens

You were already small. I think, though,
Maybe we were never close enough, as now
You're peering from the cold snap in my hand.

In the New House

I never thought of how it felt to her.

My mother had a stroke—
one arm was dead, one leg in a calipre.

And all the words she ever spoke
fell on the floor and broke.

Five months she was away.
I went to school and out to play,

and by the time that she came back
she leant to one side and was slack.

My stutter joined with hers
so when we spoke

our words lay broken all over the house.

The Smaller Picture

I'd hate to go back there—
cramped space of childhood,
square mile, the small house and school,
cramped space of knowing
bounded as though a fence
surrounds it all, and I must grow
to see above it: smallness
ties me to the ground, I can't
remember there being a sky:
grain of paving, carpet pattern,
tarred stones of the road, the grids,
council estate with fields behind,
grey grass, and bushes with thorns
and red berries I couldn't name—
I knew I was a boy, but not
what class we were, or how
my family fitted with others,
like a map pushed up
close against my eyes,
no sense of where the streets might lead
to others, and the cars to roads
and places the TV harbours—

and if I wanted to return
to feeling like that
I'd stare closely at the ground:
grass blade, dog turd, millipede.

Superman and Lois

Superman

I grow so hard
switched on by a night frosty and starred

my hard-on hauls me across the sky

I gaze out through the window of my hard-on
gasping I'm so high
and push on deeper and burst the sky

and hurtle light years into the night
hauled by the burning engines of my hard-on
gripping its tow-bar grimly tight

hauling me back before before
my mom and all
haunting me like kryptonite

until a sudden garden
brightens like a shimmering shore

which only hardens my hard-on

and I know that when a man longs
not knowing for what or why
this is what he's longing for

which only hardens my hard-on

women all fingers and cunning tongues
leaves aromatic swooning grasses
women all unguents or palpable gasses

only harden my hard-on

how they can be so many shapes
and all the universe is now this garden

and I can be this only one shape
like a wish come true I can't escape

Lois

It's being a woman or a writer
makes me so identify
with everybody in the news

including the corpses, I might tear
and open to the sky,
the buzzing buildings, hectic sidewalks and so lose

myself and shiver inside like water
with other places.
Watching superman fly
I know the currents and clouds that would confuse

me with their dizzy drift
are driven aside by his bullet resolve,

but watching I'm torn as a feather
falling then scattered in the updraught.

I, myself, and what I'm thinking of involve
and tangle together

as though today this new artist's
drawn me baffled by my features.
My face is like a vacant lot.

I'm cut off at the knees and wrists.
And robots and villains and alien creatures
go crowding into my silhouette.

Superman

I found an alien substance
always changing shape

that made me grow but also shrink
withered my powers with a glance

an alien being all agape
like a thing that's all a chink

and I read on its label
ADULT HUMAN FEMALE

and all I know is
I can punch my way though granite

Lois Lois
I am super-bodied and able

only this is where I fail
Lois Lois

my eyes could enter and seize
all the bodies on the planet

But wherever I go is
only ever Lois

whatever my eyes seize
only her aliases

Superman

I started to suspect the moon
is a fascinating woman and pale

and secretly her gravity
will undermine all men

will nightly conspire with earthly water
and every earthling daughter

always secretly on the pull

and so I wanted to transform the moon
into a solid dependable man

and hurtled up to do the Op
but hurtled *through* and couldn't stop

finding she was just a shimmery
image like a memory

and tried again and turned around
but found nowhere any solid ground

and then was pierced by a tremor
like fear for the first time of flight

nearing the source of the trouble
and bursting through her light

to find behind her glamour
only a desert of rubble

Lois

I was falling from the 50th floor
past all the flashing windows of Metropolis

like frames in which an action is cartooned.
Hard to remember who I was before

I fell from such height into such bliss:
that driven reporter, feisty, self-contained

who fell out of the sky into Superman's arms
like a baby swept up by my father.

We rise and hover and gaze down like a raptor
and see the ocean's urge to drown the shore

and the light that spurts from shuddering storms—
I've never, on a first date, gone further.

Cold light shifts across the rooftops of Manhattan,
flickers into strangeness the office where I work,

draws me, shivery, to its outlandish pattern.
Watching with the eyes of my alien captor

all I lived in day by day transforms:
the neon, the Coca-Cola sign, the *Walk/*

Don't Walk, I seldom looked up at the sky
and now I'm standing in it, like a metaphor

had gotten real that said that we could fly
if we believed enough in love's ecstasy—

I'm held up by my headspin like a helicopter.

Superman

A human swapped me, by a trick,
my body for his—

slack shoulders, creaky neck and knees,
slow dribble from his little dick.

I grow inside him, fill him up,
grow and grow and can't stop

bulging against his boundaries,
and this I'd never known before—

to feel myself to be a weight,
or walls without a door:

guilty this is one of many me's,
my disunited states—

I have no core,
I spread out like Los Angeles...

He talks like me, my parasite,
before this planet's eyes: the press, T.V.,

and wears my Clark Kent specs and suit.
But worse, *below* this,

wears my selves where I am most me,
unwrapping my Lois—

till she knows *this*
is not a superhero

by his smell...

then, like a frog kissed by a prince,
I'm woken by Lois from the spell.

But I am haunted ever since
we swapped our faces

by cravings that confined me:
corn dogs, tobacco, porn—

my strength sapped, my flight slowed, by traces
of a stranger that remind me

my self is torn
and I must drag this creep behind me

Lois

It's how he makes himself up—

his soaring away, his hurtling descent,
his boots, his pants, his vest, his cape.

Like making a person out of Lego
or writing yourself like your own author:

all action like a verb, no gap,
the opposite of hesitant Clark Kent;

no *or*, no *either*,
that *S* on his chest his own logo.

Till this comic strip,
this trick by Lex Luthor

strands him undressed in this buzzing square
as though the world of human hurt

he intercepts to wear
on himself had turned him inside out

like a t-shirt
to show the dull reverse of his image.

It's too intimate,
seeing him so limp, so slack,

and turns me touchy as a bruise
staring into his damage

as though he opened a crack
that showed his whirring clockwork

and the dark secret of his bearded back.
I grow all tender to him like a bruise—

but worry as well this being weak
is just another brief disguise.

Superman

A superhero—and polite!

But how I want to burst free
hearing from all sides in the night
women's shouts of hurt ecstasy—
I taste their cries and touch their scent

provoking this surge in me
and my selves into argument.

I wash my car. I fix a leak.
I shine my shoes. I tie my tie.
Inside I'm hiding, like Clark Kent,
the power that grips me like a freak.

But how I want to burst free—defy
the army and the FBI,
and humans who are stupid and weak,
and spill across the 'papers:

carving graffiti in the sky,
King-Konging from the skyscrapers—

free as a public enemy
or one of mine, a wicked funster—
Mentalman or Sister Freeze,
Lex Luthor or Miss Rule.

But how I need to stay cool:
slot myself inside the boundaries,

grinning like a civil monster.

Superman

Off and on it's much too much,
being so powerful makes me sick:
X-ray vision, multitudinous touch
and even the tiniest most distant tang
in my chocolate mousse of garlic
screams on my tongue.

My supersenses open me wide
so all this alien planet
haunts me with its smells and noises
living where I ought to be inside:
each odour in turn, each cry—I *am* it,
swarming with everything, and no choices.

Lois' face is crawling with mites,
others are munching sperm in my bed.
What should be me is all of this instead,
scrawling the air with millions of flights
until I back away and sink my bulk
slack across the vast US of A and sulk

hearing the billion talkers demand
hearing their need I can't escape
until I wall up in my arctic bunker
wanting not to help or understand
but be alone and sleep inside my cape
like any other wanker

The Café Bar of Rejection

Your body rejects the alien sown
inside your teenage being
whose rushes and plummets aren't your own
but you and *it* disagreeing.
Or maybe suddenly three unknown
keys are dangling from your keyring.
Love and loathing make you want to hide
and anger at your new Inside

and boredom at what adults are
and how you seep obsess and burn
out in the open in this café bar
whose staff as you approach will spurn
you like you're playing air guitar,
or squeezing your strange keys as if to turn
yourself into the one who opens
all the doors to where it all happens.

Fully Explained

Where's it come from this obsession,
aimed so far from a fuck?
This love hardly at all a fleshy one:

not love more like aggression,
wanting to bite and scratch and suck.
Where's it come from this obsession?

Love as single-minded as a session
drinking clean around the clock
thinking it's just a fleshy one:

the self I thought was my possession
lost in always thinking *Fuck* :
where's it come from this obsession? -

turning the key in my damp ignition,
spinning my wheels although I'm stuck
on love hardly at all a fleshy one:

so I say to my shrink in our session
while he probes a hairpin in my lock,
repeating, *It's this big early Lack...* —

that's where it's come from, my obsession.

Saturday Night Revisited

I've always loved this city centre
and in my teens discovered
it's volatile
and at night can invent a
whole new identity
or at least a new style
as if the city uncovered
from inside itself another city.

Offices withdraw into shadow,
stores are empty except for mannequins,
the workers and shoppers go
and some come back to shop for spouses.
I'm divorced and back, it's eight years since
I used to come. Eight years ago
I'd not have frowned at the store windows,
their lounges in impossible houses

fixed where no-one feels at home,
where tramps slump and transients rent a
brief expensive room
and Banking and Insurance
riddle the centre
with the names of foreign parts.
This club again. The old feeling restarts
in me. I drink enough so the currents

on the dance-floor carry me away
where my youth's refashioned
by samples and mixes
so now is mingled with before
and the music dissolves the floor
I'm standing on, this floor of today
and opens stories downwards, partitioned
like *then* and *now* and *maybe*, unfixes

me like wishing or regret.
And then... I'm only polite
to a fat boy who shouts at me through his sweat
but I'm pulled into a fight
and bloody the nose in self-defence
of his girl, and break a nail and lose a lens.
I sit one-eyed and pissed at my table
loving it here where it's unstable

and dread the all-night buses
circling now through the darkening outskirts
on their tour of houses and spouses
chosen for life on such little basis,
and wish I could stay
here at this table
where it's all as changeable
as a store-window display

though my ears are numb and my eye hurts

as if I could uncover
from inside myself another person,
keep shopping for another version
of myself and another lover,
seat myself on a store-window settee
hand in hand with a mannequin,
keep swapping my identity
and all I've been.

For in the Picture Sat a Plywood Gap

Smiling like moonlight over its brood
Of homes there sat a motherly, gigantic face.
I was a baby when I felt it fade
And cried at all the leftover space
And cried that there were only toys and food:
Perhaps it's always there, the sense something's ended—
Or did it start then, as my sight extended?

For now a crucial piece had been jigsawn
From the picture—like the loss of depth a wall
Confronts your look with when its mirror's gone,
Bringing you up sudden and short; for all
Dwindled in the mirror down to one.
Above the blocked hearth the wind's room muttered
And ached, as if the absence uttered.

For in the picture sat a plywood gap,
A perfect fit, its tenon precise, and its mortise—
A precious memento someone has let slip
Into a dustbin, causing fruitless sorties
To the dead harvest of the refuse tip—
Under the gulls scavenging at dusk
Picking through eggshell, empty tin, dry husk.

I entered the room searching but forgot
What for: it seemed the object of my search
Was there like an object in its name, and not.
Baffled I was tugged towards that place which,
When the plug's dislodged, tugs at your foot;
Which—as the negative in dreams (wrote Freud)
Does not exist—must be a place and not a void.

A place that's like the moment of transition
Where we always live and never settle;
Like moving house, the endless incompletion—
Nowhere to sit. stacked chairs and lost kettle—
Neither continuity nor supersession
In the waiting van, stirred dust or packed cases,
But both mingled differently in different places:

Enormous sky and plough land flat as sea,
The white horizon riddled with a hole
By a dark figure shaped to take a key.
An explanation close. Or here, where I stroll
Watching cloud shadow massively
Rising; landscape,. for no reason, a brief whole;
Cow pasture, beeches, flies hanging in the heat—
Only today these make me feel complete.

Undercurrents of Easter

Sleepless in her lounge two flights
below sea level, I remembered nets
and starfish on the club's floor,
rudders on its ceiling. Bleary headlights
undulated in her window through a flaw
spattered by a week's rain, and cars floated past
under the fish-bowl's surface upside down.
The dance-floor girls swam by the ottoman
she left me to—their lipstick ovals pursed
and widened, pursed and widened, miming, caught
in nets and jostled to a beat.
Moonlight in her mirror that raindrops dispersed
was like a chink of water bright with spawn—
faces in windows, lunes that germinate
in lit facets of pint glasses.

I'm threatened by water but immersed
in a bowl of air. A fat tide rises
fizzing with spume and curving with hips.
I think of her forbidden room as the dawn's
pullulating; at the roadsides, lips
wriggling in pavements tickling the wet
pavements pink; gardens
overgrown and dripping, grume fat
on their climbing, bushy awns;
enormous eggs in the brooding stores.
Oh let my hand grow and undo the flats
that are zipped up the middle with lit stairs!

Sultry

I'm thoroughly empty and dozing
and the drone of your vibrator

is a light aircraft circling
high on a thundery afternoon

where the parched view from its window
stretches almost

to where the sea rippling
is a troubled unreachable shimmer

From *How We Met*

It could be love

or only a bad cold turning him to water,
                its roots in his throat
tickling and its wet petals opening in his nose,
                or mostly height and rain
now he's risen to the nineteenth floor, these changes—
                love, promotion—
glazed at lunchtime, he looks out on the prospect
                of versions of himself
looking out on windows in a series all reflecting
                wall-sized windows,
wavering buildings standing in the sky,
                translucent walkers
through a glinting labyrinth turning into water—
                it could be love
or only how his rheumy vision wanders out
                into global glass
melding him and here with Sydney and New York,
                Paris and Shanghai

Sideways at the War

I noticed glancing sideways
    In the corner of my eye
A war was flashing and smoking
    And I'd forgotten why.

The war had turned into a thing
    That made itself at home
And lost itself inside my sight—
    A cup a bed a phone.

I watched it sometimes thinking
    It's supposed to make me safer,
Turned away and it slipped from me
    Like deep into the sofa,

Lodged itself in a crevice
    Mostly keeping shtum,
Was harboured in that darkness,
    A pen a pin a crumb.

Those things get lost together
    And change when they combine,
Once out of mind they differ
    And feel no longer mine.

The thought of war goes missing
    And joins a personal shame
And when I turn to face it
    The face has changed its name.

The sun is glinting on metal
    When the bedroom door's ajar,
And through the cracks in the floorboards
    I can hear an aching bazaar

For foreign bits and pieces
    Are scattered around my home,
They spilt across my carpets
    From the TV and the phone,

A whisper climbs from the plughole,
    The window's on the blink
As souks and mountains shimmer
    In sidestreets of how I think

I'm all at sea then worried
    My house is edged with elsewhere
So who I am when I'm at home
    Is neither here nor there:

But the war slipped from my fingers
    As I walked down the street,
My mind was in demand
    From someone I had to meet,

And the traffic was very noisy
    And a window flashed with screens,
It scattered me all over
    To be inside so many scenes,

For even on that corner
    The worldwide twitched its web,
But the war's allure was fading
    Like a broken celeb

The Scaremonger

I almost bought it. But that colour of mourning,
fleshly blue—it put me off. His creatures were crowded
behind the glinting glass where you could point at them,
huddled beside their heaped shards of ice with printed labels:
chilly names and points of origin, exotic and mundane.
The jaw had dropped on mine, its eyes had seen so much
they couldn't shut: they stared at the walls which were buff
and plain as the envelope his leaflet hid inside.

He knows so much we don't, he reads the codes we can't
and suffers on our behalf. His wakeful knowledge
wears away at him but his cadaverous glamour
stares from our screens and huddles of the famous
where he's safeguarded by the network and endorsed.
His stores have slipped in almost unseen on the high street.
His agents fly to all the major capitals,
they move through airports briskly with their samples.

The price, he says, is *vigilance*, but when you pay
the change he gives you plants itself in your pocket,
biding its time in the warm dark. You dwell on his logo: eyes
watching a careless back, and how it's carried by his vans
nightly, daily, down arterial roads and city streets
delivering his goods. I had to leave,
then stood below his air-vent breathing his sickness out
among the queasy takeaways and warm exhaust.

Postmodernism, Or,

I lost you in the nineteenth century
and going back was terribly hard:
the tangle of Pollocks too dense
to penetrate, the Rothkos so serene
they stopped my steps and all my striving.
History looked too changed this way around,
unlearning computers, blinding the TVs
after the flames retracted and the planes
unstuck themselves from those high floors.
What decade had enveloped you?
The prospect of reliving modernism
scared me, quickening that Loss—a dead
tree, so painful, when its numbed fingers
tingle, recoiling from the cruel flow renewed.
I swam against the tide from the shallow end
of the gallery into the old depths
past a group, mechanical, of students
copying a flat atrocity,
and women who come and go
talking of phallo- and phallogo-.
I was on a mission now, a quest,
impelling me through epochs like rooms
where light and water flickered and the Cloud
was thinning the further I travelled
so the Presence was pressing through until
it pained me with its heat and glare.

Grey Areas

The web of my novel broke
and wasn't a web any more
but fog thickening.

I took a walk. The road was white
as a margin: lights
levitated from the valley.

Lucy drinks some full-fat milk, but then
it leaves a sticky cloud
in Michael's throat—

the colours of my characters
kept running
one into the other.

The council estate was hidden, but from there
dreams billowed through me like dissolving
walls on a foggy motorway

while baas rebounded
down the wooly corridor.
The road was blank as a mind

with sudden entrances—a black-leather
seated creature with a bright
speeding navel, for example—

all my wishes and fears
went walking and talking
like people blurring into one

and I remembered I was
swallowed by a shadow
pursuing me once, or

slowly enveloped
like the willowherb
invaded from their roots,

their bottom halves all fog—
so fertile
they pale into ghosts.

And then I found a field
humming with the fog's edges:
tufts of wool on barbs
and on the gorse and thistles
grey areas like corners
closing on the flies.

Squawks and Speech

                Only the parrot observes
his body beside the futon where he tumbled.
        Hello, she calls, and again *Hello*—
                a voice on a cut-off phone—
                      and *Come Back Peter*,

            calls as though to the voices
and music from downstairs of the lonely TV,
        or blackbird near the window where words
                extend themselves through the wire
                      under its solo.

            She perches on the spread map
on the table, squawks, and waddles into the sea
        off Anglesey, her *Come Back Peter*
                as though she's searching for where
                he might be really.

            Her hunger surprises her,
the cold withering of habitat that started
        when Peter changed from upright to flat—
                a tree in the rainforest
                      that echoes briefly,

            thunders across silent miles
then joins the endless cycle of decay and growth.
        But Peter stays the same, as rush hours
                pass him by both ways, and buses
                circle around him.

            Most days the door's beak opens
and emits, not cries, but letters and newspapers
        that sprawl in heaps like speech that tumbles
                from a mouth onto the ground
                unheard and lies there—

            echolalia from outside
repeating his name as though trying to recall
      Peter, who he is, and how he fits
            into the network of roads—
                  he's a missing piece,

            lost in a room like a mind
with a memory that over and over returns,
      a phrase that recurs and calls his name
            in a tone that's not his own—
                  a stuck interior

            where the clock is sweeping through
a single season though pollen now is mingling
      with the dust on its face, and sunlight
            edges across Peter's brow.
                  The year is tilting

            and Peter's eyes are open
so the cat returning squints and mews at his lit
      irises, while, buffeting the casement,
            gusts cry their one syllable
                  of a cross baby.

Folie à Deux

The law, when their deductions falter,
call on your psychic powers.
Out of the handkerchief and key
they leave you feelings filter
through you or spread like spores
and change you like their colony.
These pieces of a killer
dropped at his scenes of crime
echo a phrase in you that's not yours,
arouse an odour, a colour,
skew you out of your own time.

You want to sit still in your own life
but in the distant rooms of summer
the killer sweats, digests and thinks
and flickers in you as you drive
and hourly in your work as a plumber
eyeing pipes and drains, their slimes,
your shadow in the worried glaze of sinks.

His stride wrongfoots your stride.
The handkerchief that nestled by his crotch
bobbles like a small loose cloud
above the pavements to his crimes.
It wraps you in its foreign weather
mingling fluids like a fuck
remembered in a semi
opened by the key,
desires you feel together.

His voice is lodged in you and smells of scotch.
It skews you out of your own place
as though your semi shook
with shouts and then the joining wall were
closing in and pushed you to one side
and you were growing smaller
and flattened like a dummy
buried alive in a case.

Fallen Women #1–7

An ear, a breast, a fluttering leg,
I search for them and make them whole.
I'm also broken like an egg,
Runny, quirky, and I want control.

Like something I can't *quite* remember,
Pieces fly from me but are a clue
Shivering in raw December.
I make a woman with my glue.

When was it women fell apart?
The legs in subways, bums in trees.
I pick them up. My healing art
Makes only smiling amputees.

I'm always missing the single piece
I rummage restlessly to find
In droppings, feathers and torn fleece,
While eyes observe me from the wind.

Last week I watched my hand escape
Through meadows open like a breach.
It might construct a fuller shape
Grasping at things out of my reach.

Misconceiving

So many reasons why you shouldn't
    pine for her, the new recruit:
the seventeen years between you, and the wife and kids you love;
    the prospect of suspicion, dispute—
        and you couldn't
    tell her, chance a move.

She's foreign to you and attractive as a niche
    Shadowy in bright cloud, a fading arch.

How many nights now you haven't slept
    but thrown your thoughts toward her
over the river, roads, and the towering city centre
    leaping beyond yourself, that border
        where you've been trapped
    and where you invent her—

A sudden alarm, or free fall off the edge
    Into sleep, a falling short and yearning bridge.

Desire like this resembles loss,
    the seventeen years a waste,
the careful repeated investment in home and career
    building a sense of self—all erased,
        not giving a toss,
    just wanting her near—

Traffic flowing the wrong way, a bridge reaching
    Never to touch, sinews taut with stretching.

How stale these Cheshire lanes have grown,
    the trees repeat their sentences,
thoughts left standing on corners start to rot, a decade
    of looking has heaped up from glances
        into fields stuffed with green,
    with all you've done and said.

Vertigo in a long window, aching stretch,
   A fissure that opens on vistas, shining catch.

   Your wife begins a secret grieving
      over what feels worse than loss—
you're missing but you're here, may not, or may be found but changed:
      she lives on a border looking across—
         misconceiving,
      familiar, estranged:

The soft speaking faces caught up in a bubble
   Staring in her eyes, the dead echoes at her table.

   But she created this character,
      her husband, from pieces of him—
looks, a point of view, ignoring how it shifted, was unstable
— invented herself thinking 'I love him',
      spliced him and her, seated,
      at a table—

Till they came unstuck so in the kitchen fragments
   Fly from their faults, conjectured traits and lost figments.

Surface Impressions

Desire was haunting your crisis
And disrupted all you were.
What made you famous was impressions
Though, infesting you with voices—
Hers was one of many invasions:
How must it feel being her?

So much herself, so singular,
Not scattered by fissions
Into sportsmen, rock stars, politicians—
Not flickering, intermittent.
Practicing one day a fresh mutant,
Briefly in the mirror you were her:

The breathy voice and dirty wit,
Feminist scorn, parodic wiggle.
Gorgeous ! Hopeless ! Two-faced tit !
All your own words caught up in struggle
As mimic and victim concur—
The face and voice, both neither you nor her.

But tied up with your crisis
Was shock at how your jokes would couple
What should be single, breeding crosses
Mingling yourself with things and people
Till you pined for something singular
And pure, and thought it was her.

Famous voices, but also the babble
From suburbs, hobbies, pubs and jobs
Fell on your wincing, obsessive ears.
Off the street you picked up dry pink gobs
And worked them with your tongue into bubbles
Speaking like all the hims and hers

In cityscapes of wanting, hoping—
All the accents in mouths that water
Over mannequins and travel brochures,

Sucking at cigarettes or straws,
Or twisted in orgasmic shopping:
Wanting and wanting, but not her—

The working jaws, the hungry registers.
Phones rang in your mouth, or the echo
Of desires fixed you in their stucco
As a new impression froze
On your lips. Promiscuous characters,
Those words your mouth holds like a purse:
The searching smoke of both tobacco
And speech. The stubbled or lipsticked Ohs.
The thousand voices coupled with hers.

Crab Lane From the New Flats

The flat window can contain Crab Lane and more:
its blackened church, its cobbled hill that climbs
to a growing council estate. I see from here
how its boundaries, bounded by the window,
are lost in Manchester. I try to see
why anecdotes will not contain its past—
the punch-drunk boxer muttering
and shadow-punching through the streets;
the leader of the Whitsuntide procession,
retarded, strutting in army boots and bowler ;
my grandfather, who dropped a ladder on his toe,
tied a slipper to his foot, and walked to work—
five miles in the snow. Those characters are caught
between before and after as by photographs,
survive in neither. They withdraw to where they live
the years between wars as Manchester advances,
not knowing how they are to be enclosed.

How We Met

Jeremy Lamb and Sianed Shark

**Choreographer, ex-dancer,
Jeremy Lamb is 43**
(or thereabouts, looks older to me).
**Most recently he has starred
as a vampire in films and TV:
in** *Moonfang, Thirsty Dark,*
The Living Were Made of Cardboard,
and *Desires of a Necromancer.*
**All this because four years ago
he danced and sang in a video
famously with Sianed Shark**
(nice link or what?)
the singer with *Compulsion to Repeat,*
composer and musician (28).

Jeremy Lamb

... but don't you think celebs mislead
you with their stories made up in advance? ...

I'd heard their single *Vampire Trance—*
oh heal it heal it so it bleed—
not knowing how our rhyming need
would stir me up, how Ned would hurt me,
and our merging like you'd not believe.

Ned's vulgar fire I envied and her youth,
gauntness and her soft full-blooded mouth,
their hit, which hurt me, *Cruel Hot Love.*

I saw her at a fancy dress party
first out of the corner of my eye
when (this is awkward !) I was bent over
trying to revive my then lover
who had fainted.
                I was bone-dry,
creaking on my last legs, forty—
she revived me. This is the muddle
though, we meant, in *Summer Rain*, our song:
hot weeks and dust that must resist
the moistening that must insist,
the stirring to life that makes it long.
She pushed me about like a nude model,
twisted my stiff limbs—confused
me with the vampire she created
filming her sight-bite *Dancing Dead*.

We're touring now—all gigs and speed,
all bumps and blur. Our voices have mated.

I'm so tired and happy, and somewhat bruised.

Sianed Shark

Mary I call him.
                He'll say it was a joke
him at the party in his black cloak
biting the throat of that ballerina.
Then I thought there'd been a
version of him long ago
looking like him in my video
sucking the life out of my people.
Strange we're such a loving couple,
him then me each other's teacher,
dancing, composing, talking Nietzsche:

special places we can merge in
ordinary people can't imagine,
chords from other planets like a margin
flickers in the corner of their eye,
déjà vu, tasteful, Gemini—
shadowed outside you like a screen ghost.
What's always disturbed me is his taste:
his food, his wine and camp old aristo clothes,
the crossover of our mouths—
he wanted mine, its redness, fulness, shape.
Also I remember a landscape—

turn off the tape Melissa turn off the tape ....

Not the landscape of my people:
hillsides, steep. Wet slate. The chapel.
Now I'm haunted by the memories
not of my own childhood, but his:
places I've never seen like déjà vu,
an old love hurting like new,
hurting with the urge to repeat—
yearning for his broken dancer's feet
bulging biceps thighs and calves
squiggly with veins: what doubles or halves
me till his face is flushed with my youth,
till it opens redly with my mouth.

Martha Agnew and Kevin Dante

**Kevin Dante (39)
is founder of** *The Spirit's Gym*:
**'the healing regime
where fitness and prayer combine'.
The dancing career
of Martha Agnew (28)
was halted for over a year
by anorexia.
Together they wrote** *The Health Hymn,*
**'a psalm of the Light and the True Weight',
and** *Curves Are Sexier.*

Martha Agnew

I was at the top of the tree
where everyone could see me.
How could I dance and be
looming too large just to be me ?
I wanted half to shrivel
and lose control by growing so small

I could fly away—lift, swivel
and fly, but lost it in a fall,
breaking like clockwork.
Noone could piece me together
while Jerry was swallowed by his Shark.

I lay down under the weather
like a bird that's lost its spark
and couldn't work.

And I recoiled from ugly Robin Cage
whose love for me had shifted into rage.

But there are Patterns: here they filled a

gap you know? I needed repairing
so They sent a body builder,
shaped a pairing
that struck me against him like a match.
I fell in the street. Sat down, feeling fat.
He lifted me saying *You don't weigh much*
and carried me back to his flat.
I burrowed downwards through his touch
and curled myself up into nothing—
and turned myself over like a new leaf,
his easy pickup, useful, soothing
as a doll that comes to life,
knowing fame had made me man-nish.
Kevin's a saint. We can diminish

ourselves and shade into a margin
meekly, mildly, that we merge in.
That man pumped up, I imagine—
once I saw him, during a Cure
hover slightly above the floor,
and he can change, at will, my figure—
growing lighter by growing bigger.

So I smile to think one day of Kevin,
feeling a Change not steroids but like leaven
ballooning heavily into heaven.

Kevin Dante

When she was coming back from being ill
she twisted her ankle and fell.

It's shocking, the power of her will—
although she plays the underdog.

We crossed so often on our jog,
her ticking over like with anger.
I watched her burning with hunger
flustered and all aslant,
taken by what she must want.

That day was cloudy but the sky
opened, where she fell, one eye,
like a ladder led from the sun—
the time was quick with time, like soon
and once and after all in one.

I touch, and Something intercedes.
The hands on Matha's clock unfroze.
A store sang *heal it till it bleeds*.
A mystery altered our clothes
we stumbled through in search of leads
 straps and supports and springy shoes,
networks of sweat, our rhyming creeds—
baggy tracksuits alive with clues.

But Jeremy Lamb, that camp liar
had written himself all over her skin—
everywhere I could feel where he'd been:
Jerry, who hides that he's a vampire
by hamming it like a role.

He won their struggle for control,
taught her to fly and set her on fire.

And I was left to make her whole
and clear the traces of his message
and the stigmas of her hurting role
with herbs, aromas, weights and massage:

Scapegoat, burning bird and dancing doll,
Jerry shaped her in his vice
until she thought she was that girl
Winter wants as a sacrifice
and dances till her body gives,
dances herself into the ground
till all of Nature lives.

And she fell in love with her own wound.

Jag Leppard and Robin Cage

**Publicity agent
Jag Leppard rose to fame
because Jane Crook attacked him by name
in Parliament,
abusing, some said, her 'privelege'.
His motto is *The Truth Varies*.
Sianed Shark and Robin Cage,
the escapologist,
have gained from the deft twist
he's given their stories.**

Jag Leppard

I want to see the text of what I say
before it goes to print OK? ...

You know this: times your self-image
fogs, the contrast flattens,
colour drains from your screen?
They saved my sanity, did Cage
and Dante who showed me Patterns
composing the picture unseen—
Kevin's a saint, or health sage
and healed me till I knew my needs
were not my wants,
                but Robin's dwarf
height and thick specs are camouflage
his will so far exceeds
his bounds of body, casts his slough
of self—he's ... well, a sort of mage.
And days had been too much the same with me
and then the same. He makes things differ
from what they are and as my model
healed me with his manly alchemy:
the wet same days grew sharper, stiffer
straightening their damp muddle ...

Words can wriggle free—
manly is not the one you want,
Melissa there.
           I teach my clients
words, handcuffed, straitjacketed,

still sidle and slither into print
and shape them with that violence
where lives get marketed—
but Robin evades every curb:

no-one believes he was at
the party where we met;
he brims with himself like a verb
and *is* all at once and then he's not,
all out of reach of regret.

He argued with Ms.Shark, that hard babe,
shouted *Fuck it's finished*—
and I loved his dismissive flair
so much—then climbed into a wardrobe,
bellowed some curses and vanished,
flickering in the mirror on its door.

Robin Cage

He said that? Well with Jag it was a struggle ...
The key, Melissa, is to change
and break and enter and burgle
the beings of others and grow strange—
down to each thinking click and gurgle
even to yourself and change your shape,
your only habit to escape.
But Jag got stuck
with Sianed fixed in his sight
himself all pointed at a fuck,
his string drawn back endlessly tight.
I saw him at Compulsion first,
the band, staring like he was stuck fast.
We talked. He felt ignored
like a tap running till he poured
out of himself in search of her:
Sianed the siren, Jag the temptee
till he blanked his character,
leaking till he was empty ...
That's the fourth, Melissa, no wonder ...
No. Whoever looks at you must know this ...

Well I took him home and put him under,
started to heal him with hypnosis
(as I could for you, for your nicotine,
your nails, your eating, — could remedy them).

Thing is, Jag's refashioned what I've been
to TV, the papers, he's my medium,
changed what I am into a role
to show the public what it can mean
to change and escape. He took control
and I flourished in his image ...

No, it's true — what Sianed stole,
I wanted to repair that damage,
how he walked like a lost soul
inside his grey suit ... I was his mage
only in restoring him, his inner —

but meet me at *The Blank Page*
at nine, if you like, and we'll have dinner.

Jane Crook and Grace Rose

**'The male desire for victims haunts
this vilifying of Grace Rose,
the slanders, the jokes and the taunts.
How sadly her case shows
that male frustration vaunts
itself as moral rage.'** —
**The junior minister
Jane Crook is 44.
She's battled** (in this sort of prose)
**for over a year
to clear the name of the star
of soap and stage**
(who lies about her age).

Jane Crook

One of the media's versions of her
shocked me: that she was a sick mimic—
phones you as your dead mother, lost lover ...

not the others: handcuffs, pills, bulimic ...
bull dyke ... that famous chef, her recent ex
who claimed she gobbled pork out of his wok,
tied him up with his own socks,
chucked up over his cock
and force-fed him fried pork and sex.

The empty eyes of the whole culture
spread her out above us
while our hungers like a vulture
picked at her body between our covers.
When I saw her for the first time live
she swooped and soared above the stage ...

Peter Pan ... all that demand to believe ...

and just in front, with this strange look, Robin Cage ...
sorry, I was struck—my daughter who's five
gasped as she flew. We went backstage
and met this frightened little girl, this Grace
bewildered as though each hostile image
flickered like sun and cloud across her face
until she settled like a screen—

and then her shoulders tightened,
she deepened her voice, and I was watching all I've been
in TV interviews (slightly cheapened)
earnestly explaining what I mean.
She told me—as myself—what it was like
to be confused with images of her
as though her fantasies could leak
and make her guilty as her own voyeur.

Twelve million pricks with Grace in their sight
perked up and pointed, which aroused my anger

that what's desired gets hurt by spite,
and how we're changed in the eyes of a stranger.
Her frailty made me stronger:
I wanted to hold the boy in flight
as though my arms had caught a
briefly pure thing, the way a valley holds mist
or arms of land the dippy water

that can half accept them, and half resist.

Grace Rose

There's somebody sometimes
I've no antibodies for,
who maybe who they are rhymes
with something I've lost they could restore,
who then I need to follow, to know
who they are where I can't go.

Jane says it's like I'm on a tour
of where they feel themselves being
most personally, and go there sight-seeing.
Otherwise I'm stuck inside this frame
of who I am and who I am,
the picture's fixed the same and then the same.

When I project I'm freeing
myself, I'm someone at the moment when she's full
of herself like a shy boy
knowing now, YES, this is going to be,
will happen now, this gorgeous pull;
a singer watching massed bodies obey

the moves her tongue shapes and her breath,

or Martha Agnew, such control
of her blazing body it's like growth or death
or both—it tightened round me hard, that role.
I spoke and walked a year in character
and sprouted stigmata hurting like her:
bruising from Jerry, cuts she made that bled

from my arms, their veined soft turn, and my stomach.
Then I mutated like a virus and spread
across the papers like an epidemic.
Guilt, Meliss. I wanted to be punished.
Guilt. You think I'm good? I wanted to see
my image distorted and diminished,

but I got this phonecall from my MP
making a mission out of me—
Jane all furious about men and why.
I sent her a ticket to see me fly
and felt myself give toward her
for her earnest wishing to protect.
I'd curled up tight and lived in purdah,
sick of those fantasies, and worried I infect
innocent others.
                And my eating disorder,
or Martha's ? ... someone else inside you slims
and slims and says you're still not thin ...

but Jane's a bridge where the sun brims
in your face, and the colours and shapes begin
to begin ... a hundred happy whims

of shopping and cooking
and standing still and just looking
at tall buildings cars and the flickering sky
where time opens on surprised leisure ...
daily things she taught me change your stale I

with ordinary pleasure, just pleasure.

Jo Toogood and Simon Lamb

Jo Toogood's weekly column
Power of Speech
exposes hype and spin
(except her own, the two-faced bitch).
**The therapist Simon Lamb
is brother of Jeremy,
the dancer and pop star.
He helps his patients deal with fame—**
'delusions of celebrity'
**and 'gaps between the self they are
and who they are perceived to be'.**

Jo Toogood

What shouldn't, Melissa ... — its power:
turnings away gripped by a flush,
tryings so it won't appear
which DOES, and happens, then is hush hush.

I knew, before, the main stuff—
the phone-call Grace had made to Robin Cage,
half-guessing why it was enough
to start it all, his vengeful rage ...

and finding myself half in love
just muddled me up with all those names,
with Jeremy, Sianed, Martha and Jag.
I played with Si, at first, games
where yes wavers, and then a snag
because he wanted to be hurt—
it's what he does, absorb the hurt
of everybody to convert

and thrive on, and infuriate
me with his stillness, how he gapes
open gulping it all in

but when he made me free associate
linking the facts and leaping the gaps

I saw a dancer scarred and falling

from ever so high ...
                         saw a healer levitate
and look as though he knew the answer ...

saw the dwarf master of escapes
whisper in his agent's ear a luscious lie ...

a broad man watching from a margin
with blood on his chin ...

an actress who learned to fly
and turned into a dancer ...

millions of mirrors with her image in—

the press, TV, oh Grace, the travesty.

I felt empowered. Just to know
all that plot was conquering vertigo
and standing firm above the dizziness
till every wet no hardens into yes.
And know each character, and their address

and watch the gradual light open each street
and alley, and the answers lie at my feet.

Simon Lamb

'A needy obsession with *healing*'
(Jo wrote) 'is gripping the culture'

but came to me following the spoor
of Robin and what I was concealing
about my brother and Grace and Martha.

She shrank me with her looks like my mother
who always favoured my brother
and told me what I should be feeling.
Jo in my room and the others grow and grow
but change in their versions of each other.
I shrink and back off like a creature
who watches, curled up, from the ceiling

this spectacle of self, of character
like features packed tight into a box,
bound hard between their scalp and their socks
like tightly plotted books.
There's more in me of what I'm not,
no patterns, just the runny blot

and Jo and the others leave a thick growth
of words on my floor I climb through like a sloth
or shrink into like camouflage.

I tire of Jo and her lost plot,
searching the victim and the tyrant
and the sucking of blood out of Grace,
her bearing the sick collective brunt.

She hated you that night in The Blank Page
glancing over the head of Robin Cage,

me glancing back at your clever face
Melissa ...
          But your smiles are all a front.

You're all the same. Your drive for power. Your lies—
however much my need complies
with all you victimisers want
to make myself the sacrifice
and solve myself like a long haemorrhage ...

The William Ewart Gladstone Comic Strip

Part One: The Medium

The Medium: Caricature

i) Attempting a Likeness

Under the pondering detective's eye
The outline of the chalked victim on the floor
Rises and walks backwards from her fate
Into conjectured feeling and flesh.
But reconstructions lack a vital part:
Detective, like cartoonist, travesties
The full-blooded, open-eyed aliveness
Moment by moment of the victim.
Pensive, he doodles her silhouette;
Cross-hatched or limned, she is still life,
Though animated, she can hardly breathe.
Such sketches are premised on a distance
That generalises and belittles
As sun-warmed lovers, splashing and laughing, get
Reduced, a mile away across the beach,
To eight dark limbs and two dark torsos,
And a sketchy scamper like a dog.
The whole of someone else's being
Won't be grasped, but how the victim
Narrowed her eyes enlivens her silhouette—
It's otherwise so close to nothing
Rain falls through it, wind blows it out of shape.

ii) Finding Likeness in Unlikeness

The victim smiles from her photograph
But didn't look this way to her husband,
As Feiffer knew who drew a desperado
Loneliness created, plotting to murder
The telephone, his wife's true love.
What never could've happened
Can summon up what did in summary
Execution. So a dream might help me at the start—
Calm General Gordon's cockpit bucks and dives,
His dials whirr, and he ignores the politic
Control tower, where Gladstone tries to talk him down,
But watches the green of England whiten
With adoring upturned faces, and in vain
Pulls his wheel and races down to earth.

iii) Exploding likeness through rebellion

For thirty years I published my cartoons
In right-wing dailies: in the floor of print
They opened up a crack revealing
Lower stories, flammable rubbish, oubliettes.
My anger stripped complacent fat
And turned oppressors into victims: fought,
As Grosz did, fire with fire—the tall building in
His *Homage to Oscar Panizza*
Has window frames as stark as a grille—
All Hell is burning behind them;
Or they're like a woodfire's tortured
Skeleton, when, seconds-long,
A gust blows off its living surface.

Or maybe I gave comfort to my enemies.

The Medium: Comic Strip

Since my commission demands
A history-can-be-fun
William Ewart Gladstone Comic Strip,
I've had to multiply the frames:
Motion in fragments, and *fumetti*—
Those balloons for speech and thought.
Each frame's a momentary stay,
Bounding a cleared place
In which an action gets explained.
This ought to reassure, except that,
Flipping through the strips,
All those boundaries so quickly
Flickering by, upset my eyes
With what they can't digest—
Like the *moiré* effect of railings
Rippling across my windscreen
With waves behind them, crosscurrents
And what I can only guess at underneath.

The Medium: Searching for Shape

Sometimes the strips worry
how they only grow, extend—
they want to tell a single story
with beginning, middle and end

but falter ...

They want to piece the past's
body together bone
by bone, and flesh its ghosts,
each frame a stepping stone—

but water ...

and each strip is ...

Worry how the gap is
wide—the next stones disappear—
the water deep—each step is
stalled with longing like a pier
and broken like ellipsis ...

Part Two: The Strips

My First Victim

Uncle Jim was not my uncle
And he sat in my daddy's chair.
I can't believe my mother picked him.
With his gut and his carbuncle,
Stop mithering and Don't stare,
Uncle Jim was my first victim.

For I knew my real daddy was real,
But Jim had nicked him in one swallow,
Or wore him like a bad disguise.
A hole had opened in all I could feel:
Inside my dad's coat this dad was hollow,
Though my dad looked out through his eyes.

Across the Thirties great waves pressed—
The waves that run across money and land,
Half-human waves that crash and boom—
And carried Jim in his boots and vest,
Pushed him through the bowels of money, and
Voided him in our living-room.

Or Jim had marched across the land
Searching for fruitful living room,
A place where he could be in charge
And let his gut and dick expand:
A kitchen and impressionable womb
Which he could rule by being large.

Some childish premise that expects
Power to be rational and just
Recoils from the crushing weight
Of its damp haunches and connects
The thrust for more with greed and lust—
Sleek cheeks that chew on the State.

So Jim became my prototype
For power and all its alien works:
The whirling wheels and cogs and teeth
Or cunning intestines, quaking tripe,
The monster machine that lurks
Flagrantly inside, beneath.

Too flagrantly. For politics
Is not a body with its drives,
And power's diffuse or unaware:
Its corridors grow blind, unfix
Themselves, are tangled in our lives
But step out abruptly high in the air

Or run down muttering into the ground.
For power slips between the hard lines
Cartoonists draw, evades the frame
Where physical obsessions confound
Personal and political designs,
Pull down the pants of public shame—

Simplistic gesture of rebellion.
Anger at Jim squeezes my eyes,
The simple static fact of greed.
But when I switch the telly on
Power flickers, all its shapes are half-lies,
Shifting, dissolving, like the blur of speed.

The Elastic Band

England became an elastic band,
stretched itself further and further
over raw mountains and whelming sand,
heathen terrain and primitive weather,

frayed its elastic on craggy peaks,
snagged it on jungles, soaked it in seas,
hacked at by Afghans, hacked at by Sikhs—
always and everywhere, new enemies:

These few, these happy few, this band of brothers,
this band could play *God Save the Queen*,
taught the tune to exotic races
but heard in their own thoughts those others
mix a strain of English which would mean
the elastic snapped back in our faces.

Young Dog, Young Cat

The young dog Gladstone
Wears a shiny-bright dog-collar
But it looks as though
His fallen halo's tightened at his neck;
His brow is broad and noble, but
Subverted by his flexing nose—
A connoisseur of dubious breezes,
He tests them, tests them in his vast nostrils ...
The young cat Disraeli clings
To the greasy pole; his claws slip,
He clings ... then tries again,
Losing some claws on the climb.
He's gracile but ferocious,
Domestic but exotic.
Husbands beside snoring wives
Half-envy his bright nights
Conjectured beyond their bedrooms,
Envy, too, the risky days—
Trap him in a corner
He'll houdini out,
Pin him down, he'll vanish
Limb by limb, leave only
A translucent smile

A Beast Fable

Disquiet at one edge of the frame, and then

This blind tunnelling beastling emerges
From a dimlit turn in a winding sentence,
From a devious alley under plausible ground.

Gladstone stumbles on it in the small hours
In his kitchen. It reminds him of dark
Doodles in illuminated books
Infringing from a margin on a reading eye;
Gargoyles leaning into conversations;
Carved horrors under his seat at prayer.

He met it first when, as a boy, following
A fairy tale, he missed the point and found
The wrong path.

                It's like a buried memory
Surfacing through a hole in the nursery floor
But scattering by chairs and tables

Tumps of dust and must from tenements,
Of papers, books and keys from counting-houses,
Secrets from pockets, chests and strong rooms.

So as he looks into the deep
Recesses in its head, its tunnel vision,
He sees the secrets he suspected there —
Which reassures him.

                But then he glimpses

Tunnels branching from the near tunnel,
Shadows of worries and secrets not familiar
But further concealed and still unworried.

An Enchanted, Perverted, Topsy-Turvy World

'We have much studied and much perfected, of late, the great civilised invention of the division of labour ; only we give it a false name. It is not, truly speaking, the labour that is divided ; but the men:- broken into small fragments and crumbs of life ; so that all the little piece of intelligence that is left in a man is not enough to make a pin, or a nail, but exhausts itself in making the point of a pin or a nail.'
—Ruskin

'It is an enchanted, perverted, topsy-turvy world in which Monsieur le Capital and Madame la Terre do their ghost-walking as social characters and at the same time directly as things.'
—Marx

As Ruskin sketched his still life *Sloes*
Anatomising stem and leaf,
A creature scurried across the ground —

An old hand like a detail
Extracted from a master,
A life-like hand and moving
Like a spider on its finger-tips.

It was a calloused factory-hand —
A man or woman much reduced.
For what a piece of work was Man!
A piece-worker now, a work in pieces.

So I've dismantled a working-man,
My frames like mirror fragments;
Jagged edges holding here
A narrowed eye, a tensed elbow; there
A flexed knee, a turning wrist.

But when these pieces assemble,
People are cannibalised in things:
Since men have mated with matter
The misbegotten are on every hand.

Chimeras, monsters of desire:

A balustrade of knobbly knees
A spoon that hides a gargoyle in its face

A chest of drawers

An arm-like pier whose reach exceeds its grasp
A shelf of swells with one akimbo arm

A chest of drawers that's banged up tight

The thick black thought of the smokestacks
Hardening on churches and town halls

A woman with a floral cover, hand-sewn,
Suspension and curled hair in her seat,
Who reaches out, with sharp desire,
Upholstered and enfolding arms.

Brother and Sister

'Sequestered once more as her father's companion, Helen lapsed into depression and hysteria. The doctors prescribed laudanum and alcohol as tranquillisers. She was soon addicted ... Probably Gladstone was only too aware of how near he himself could come to the kind of breakdown which overwhelmed his sister. All his life he had been aware of powerful and intense passions being restrained only by a rigidly systematic self-control.'

Richard Shannon, Gladstone

This strip is only two frames wide
And oddly one-sided.
Light shines into the right,
On William: only his shadow falls
On Helen, in the left.
The two frames are windows running,
Adjacent, down a tall building.
The left's an ante-room of history
Where Helen listens at the wall —
For in the right there's Church and State
And William's mind aloft
Soaring over his winged collar;
The left's a woman's place
But topsy-turvy — deranged
Furniture, and food
Meeting on plates like a mad
Association of ideas.
Also the left opens
On the claustrophobic expanses
Of a laudanum dream:
A staircase, then another
Winding higher into the dark.
She glances up and sees herself again
Five staircases higher
Gazing down into an abyss.

Romance. Hysteria. Opium.
Yet the passions that consume Helen
Only stoke William up,
Driving him on.
He pushes back, intrepid,
The frontiers of the dark left,
Bringing light from the right.

So it's odd that the right
Weakens now, and William's thoughts
Bubble up in the left;

That light, behind his back,
Has circled round and shines
Redly from the left;

That right and left converge
And form a stereoscope—
Together the two embody
Fully-rounded figures,

And when Helen is on top
Of the staircase looking down
She sees a collar beating its frail
Wings above the abyss.

Re-Animator

After the past's re-animation
Collages blood and nerve and gland,
It's back with a hitching motion
Touching the present with the cold hand,
For instance, of Gladstone's mission,
Pacifying Ireland.

But the past is a body dismembered
Or series of stills with serious gaps
So heavily encumbered
With wishes and fears and perhaps
Its figures look half-timbered
And their animation stops.

For history stitches
Bodies together with parts
Of speech, the way my pencil cross-hatches
A past my present distorts,
A hybrid time whose lost arm itches,
Hybrid longing that reverts,

Searching the present for the past
To heal the gulf between,
Missing a remembered breast
Or piece of ass, to dwell on gaps that mean
We can survive in pieces by moving fast,
Pulling ourselves together scene by scene.

Rescue Work

He sails the good ship *Rescue*
for London is a tossing sea
where girls are bobbing.

The yonder is wild and blue:
although I know he wasn't me
hearing those calls, that sobbing,

I know his pent-up torrents
ached, bewildered his mission,
as though a fear and a wish

rocked his ship with cross-currents,
all my frames with double-vision.
He can hear her: half a fish,

and half a lady, she calls in the night
where paving, tarmac, brick dissolve
into these tides that waver

because he's stirred up by her plight,
swollen, straining at his hard shut valves.
His need is just to save her,

haul her up from where she's sinking —
he'll reform her once he's caught her.
Except this tantalising yonder

melts into marsh unstable and stinking
between the states of land and water
where the mud might suck him under.

An Unlikeness

My mind's been changed by this commission,
Old though I am. This is a strange position
To think of my hero in: lifting
Myself out of and away and drifting
From the girl, the car, estranged from passion,

Into darkest England and Gladstone's mission—
Saving prostitutes. She lifts my stiff hips
Deftly away—for in her fingertips
There's better knowledge than in all
Of Gladstone's conscience. She is supple and small,

Quiet now and slow, but understood the need
That drove us in the backseat with such speed.
But he was driven by obsession—
Missionary, in all except position,
To that backstreet Africa of the soul.

Once I thought he must've, merely to console,
Touched a shoulder, to encourage, squeezed a knee,
And that his hand must've held that memory
Holding his knife amidst his family
Polished and glinting as they eat and chattered.

Caricature suggests we've shattered
Our own image and our pieces have scattered:
Severed arm, evacuated longing,
Spilt content no longer belonging,
Walking finger, footloose leg—all diverge.

Gladstone I thought was severed by an urge
From his own hand: it cabinet it sketched
Monsters of desire—limned, dislimned and cross-hatched,
Begotten not by fusion but by fission,
By the contradictions of his mission.

Zips and buttons! Now we've pulled ourselves apart,
We pull ourselves together—young thing, old fart.
In draughty corners where the self shivers—
Waste ground, parked cars, brief rooms—spent slivers
Of me quiver and live; desire severs

Me from my brief selves; regrets dismember
What I was and wish and can't remember:
Pieces torn from me like scraps of girls borne
On the wind, the tits and bums of Fern and Dawn
Tortured by hawthorne or drowning in puddles.

But my searching for a likeness muddles
Me and Gladstone: continent he coasted kerbs
Content with nouns like Duty, and no verbs.
His actions and words said only what he meant,
Aloof and stiffened like a monument.

An Ill Wind

A vast nose and a turning weathercock—
Inside the nose, a rare easterly
Had turned the city back to front.
Most days the ruling ideas are borne
By westerlies to the hidden poor:
That day their poor breath fogged the wealthy streets,
Microbes with the faces of crossing-sweepers
Swarmed in drawers through lavender and rose-leaves.

The smell then entered Parliament
Representing water and air:
The Commons whitened with handkerchiefs
As though the old windbag made it weep.
Upset, the belly politic
Rumbled in the Thames, and then
The bubbles spoke in the House.

Dr. Morph and Mr. Darwin

Is it a man is it a bird?
A slug a snake a swift? Oh no:
still trailing his Darwin beard

my Morph's a blighted superhero,
longing to stay, one day, the same,
hopping in the dark of a burrow

then a curlew calling its own name,
his lips erupting in a long curved beak,
and then, just crawled out on a harsh shore,

oh no, a sickly hybrid, weak freak,
caught between two beings, all unsure,
watched by a big sky, a stormy cape.

And Darwin regrets: he never meant
his alter ego to escape,
crippled from his botched experiment.

I limn and dislimn, my cross-hatched
animations flicker like fractals.
Morph awakes this time in a scorched

canyon steaming with pterodactyls.
Now he shrivels and grows stiff,
drowning in air through his wracked gills,

cast out as an arthropod,
stuck in the face of a cliff
like a doodle by God.

Dr. Morph and Mr. Gladstone

His silhouette flickered out of line,
Would not conform, then tugged its toes from his,
Was off to live a severed life
In corners, darkening doors.

Morph flickered in Gladstone's drawing-room:
A shadowplay of life-forms
Hatching on his wall, of limned
Creatures and dislimned, of cross-hatched
Animations feuding as soon as they stir ...

But shadows crowd round Gladstone
Walking the streets of Soho—
Shadows in frock-coats, shadows in skirts,
Limned, dislimned,
The gaslight racking their shapes.

Traffic Island

Impossible, but hot and graphic,
a desert island in the traffic.

To turn a thought into a place
it's bounded as his personal space.

Around him it's all to and fro:
the bearded man's got nowhere to go.

His beard has reached his ragged knee.
It means—the island—what it means to be.

Victorians felt that starting when
so much became beyond our ken.

Beyond our ken was just a notion,
our island's threatened by an ocean.

The soul, its wherefore why and what
is all dissolved in the cannibal's pot.

No point in dwelling on what's inner,
the natives want you for their dinner.

And so I took this old cartoon,
the man alone with his thought balloon.

Since he's alone no matter where
the island's in a city square.

Expanses stare him in the face:
an ocean cramps each person's space.

Mid-century Calm

A stone names the building '1860'.
Stripping its facade reveals
A roomy framework for my strip.

The coverings on the middle storey,
Though, will not be stripped away:
The curtains, cushions, gilded tapestry,
The lady lost in crinoline,
Allegory in a fretted frame.

But in the attic is a primate
Growing frightened of himself,
His cassock shrinking from the fur
Sprouting on his hands and feet.

And in the basement of the year
The voices of the ragged are condensed
And silenced in the icy enclosure:
White fumetti from their breath
Steam to their ceiling and disperse.

I pull back slowly from the house
Letting its facade heal up around it,
And I can hear the noises start—
Polite rock music and internal combustion:
The street-scene looks quite realistic.

Napoleon's Double

'[In Napoleon III] The French ... have not only a caricature of the old Napoleon, they have the old Napoleon himself, caricatured as he must appear in the middle of the nineteenth century.'

—Marx

His father swarmed with repetitions,
Billions of little Boeys in his blood.
His mother's womb had nightmares—
Loaded with blanks she delivered
Only a genetic message:
Kevenhuller, coatee, jackboots.

Oh this engine tradenamed Bonaparte,
This whirring replica
Of cogs and ratchets: new, improved—
Press the button and he conquers Europe.

Hero for the new times, the century
Middle-aged and plump and rich;
Napoleon in a counting-house:
In court he strips to show his vest marked 'N'
And no-one notices he's naked.
But my Benday spots, ironic,
Thicken like night and Russian snow
Falling together.

Tadpoles quicken now in the gene pool,
Surface as human in delivery rooms:

Become Napoleon the car-park attendant,
Napoleon the head of Human Resources,
Napoleon pitching Minimum Death Benefit,
Flashing Napoleon in the fast lane,
Napoleon on an 18 handicap—

Piss-proud Napoleon, all his little boneys
Pushing up against a bulging fly.

I Don't Think

There's a need in nature
Now and then, a hunger
In a stretch of country,
In Flanders or near Austerlitz:
Innocent patches, tussocky
Cow pasture; young plateaux
Cut by canyons; wooded valleys
Loud with water and birds—
Hunger for human flesh.
In 1854 were shipped to Turkey
French cockerels, British bulls:
By 1856 there sat the half-
Eaten everywhere on city streets.
But if you'd looked at Inkerman
Then, that also had been eaten,
Limbless trees and chewed turf—
So whose was the hunger?

Victoria Grieving for Albert

The owl Victoria
Is hardly ever seen,
But she is heard
Haunting graveyards
Wooing the dark.
Her head swivels around
Full circle
Peering after the lost one
Behind her, lost behind.
Her moonlight shadow
Crosses the country,
Touching the people
With its cold fingers.

Dummies

I almost could identify
with Browning, how his I

through being worn
by big ideas, gets torn

or alters like many a
form imagined through millenia

quickening selves
until his I dissolves

and someone else's water in his eye
hurts him with complicity,

his I a house with changing boarders,
painting pictures and plotting murders

his I a wardrobe all bespoke
in alien sizes that bespeak

the formative but foreign babble
that crowds his I as though with scrabble

and squeezes through the mirror
a chatty chimera.

The Boy Who Turned Into a Puppet

'Civilisation has taught us to renounce cruelty and aggression which once ran riot in atrocious reality and magical practises ... In caricature, however, these forces find a well-guarded playground of their own ... With the caricaturist we may relapse into a stratum of the mind where words and pictures, rules and values lose their well-established meaning, where the king may be changed into a pear ... In the eternal child in all of us lie the true roots of caricature.'
— Gombrich, *Caricature*

My medium makes me think of childhood when I think
Of Mill, the son — as Gombrich says, it makes
The playground erupt into adulthood.
So the adult Mill, in crisis,
Had to go back — reliving like a walker
Yesterday's steps to where he pulled out,
With his handkerchief, the dropped key,

For looking back he saw a face behind his face —
His own, behind his father's: two-way personation.
All his life he'd seen through his father's eyes
Searching for happiness like a perfect
Landscaped garden. But some fairy tales come true
In a trick mirror, where they frighten you.

Look out behind you cry the children's voices —
For he frightened himself, ghosting up behind his back.
The garden imprisoned him; his mask began to rot.
I draw his arms, legs, torso, face. Like me he tried
To draw himself together, and like me he managed
Only a twisted face, a deformation of character —
There, in the trick mirror, his figure jumping.

The Two Heads of Carlyle

His two voices are like rivers—the left
Warm, green and wide, debouching
Into an ocean, but the right a force
Fast, white and cold, and disappearing
Underground. The left voice joins
With earth voices, sky voices, ocean voices—
Hymns, community singing—
To God and fellow-feeling, reaches out
To flora and fauna, to the people—
Must encompass what it cannot,
In its one-armed embrace: the right arm
Draws back, draws in. The right head listens,
Suffers; adds in brackets guilt,
Need for guidance, shouts the other
Finally down: opposes to that reaching out
The social pyramid, Necessity
Tight as the flight of a braced falcon
Simplifying itself into talons and beak,
Tightening its flight, tightening,
Sharpening itself, narrowing its sights,
Narrowing itself down into its stoop.

Making Myself Scarce

A piece of me is lost
I'm always trying to recover,
Like an unknown woman that I missed:
We would've made such perfect lovers
But she glanced in my compartment as she passed
And chose another;

A feeling in my teens I mislaid
Close to the edge of the council estate,
Beside the turn-off from the main road,
Where the path falters in a flooded rut
Shining dully from a thinning in a cloud —
It's there my right foot

Singularly paces
Feeling above it such a lack of weight,
Lonely outcast from the other pieces,
Haunting the altered council estate,
Where splashed orange in the puddles disperses
Me in the light.

Trying to remember
It's as though the scattered pieces long
For one another, and each member
Trembles for a body, trembles to belong:
A hand on a hill attempting to clamber
With its rubber fingers along

The steep, wet and dimpled paving;
Or my right foot going toe and heel —
Estranged from me, a footloose craving
I look into the hungry night and feel,
Fractured and half-twinned in the double-glazing.
How my hand on the hill

Searches blindly for me—
But expulsions and an early breach,
Or blank in understanding, tore me;
Or I broke where longing made me stretch,
For baulked desires caricature me:
I'm a talking crotch—

Urges I disown—
A foot that haunts a kerb, a hand that gropes;
Pieces with fractious minds of their own,
Like feelings in exile, a lip that creeps
Into a pavement cranny, selves thrown
Like weightless scraps

Unless by force they're drawn
Together—hand and foot and spoken fart,
And I become myself, not helplessly borne
Against my will, but framed by vengeful art—
Till who I am is made from what was torn,
By tearing others apart.

An Irish Joke

The earl smoked at his club,
his premises all ha-ha.
Inside his cloud it said,

'The Irish are niggers
white from eating potatoes.
They're animated picks and spades.
Their island hovers under ours:
a basement, badly lit,
and smelling of wet earth.
They broke the ladders we offered
and carry the rungs around as clubs.'

But Gladstone's not amused.
He feels a sudden heat
at his heels, and sees a floorboard-crack
blink with old newspapers catching fire.

Turkey, Plum Pudding

Diplomatic relations
Crowd the death bed,
So greedy to inherit
Turkey looks trussed up
Under a silver lid.

A frightened eye
Opens in the meat,
Thinking *frog* and kraut
Thinking *roast-beefs*

Thinking after Gillray:
Vulture heads of state
Carve the edible globe—
Such skill they have, the delicate
Long fingers of gourmets!

On velvet cushions, cutlery
Enters in procession.

Turkey hopes the vultures choke
On the hard riches hiding
In the soft plum pudding.

The Dark

Imagining Africa, this strip's
A ladder downward into the dark

Or black roll of film, a negative
That cannot be developed:

The mind that tries to find a way into
Dense forest, vast silence, empty stream

Recoils. Construct a jungle
Out of hothouse details,

Near and far conflated,
Flattened into far—

Find darkness again,
Shadow in intense growth,

Then Rousseau dream clearing, or desert—
Wind wiping the fine sand's memory

Of footsteps, and again darkness.
Take the ladder downward,

Find a frame that's a black window—
Nearness now, not distance

Stops you seeing—something
Pushed up, brushing your lashes:

Near and far conflated,
Flattened into near.

You're back now where you started, square one,
Though the mind that tries to find a way into

Close quarters, near starvation,
Recoils from darkest England:

Lost backstreet tribes; darkness
In the shadow of intense growth.

The Assumption

Gladstone fixes his eyes on the clouds, his ears
On murmurs of a distant sea marked 'Faith'.

Light-headed, his winged collar
Lifts him two inches, then a foot,

But his body is smoke-blackened marble,
His bag is document-heavy,

He tumbles back down.
He tries again, whispering a plea,

Yearning for above and beyond, the blue
Yonder, here a shade of grey.

The High Anglicans are less encumbered
Walking a tightrope between two steeples,

But below them, when they mount higher,
Miles have been reclaimed from the sea

And there are Punch and Judy shows
An iron tower

And further out a pier
Whose reach exceeds its grasp;

The bathers on the beach have telescopes
And watch the shining waves far off,

Paddle in shallow pools
And worship the noise in shells.

The wind blows the clouds on-shore.
A mongrel looks at Gladstone and cocks its leg.

The sky grows overcast
With mute *fumetti*.

Hatred of Gladstone

I've lived with Gladstone half a year.
I talk to him about my class
But it's as though he doesn't hear
Or thinks about them as a mass
Or blur, or sulky beast or sea
Likely to rise against his kind—
They seem subhuman, the enemy
By which we might be undermined.

But then he waxes sympathetic,
Which is worse, thinks up a worker-clone
Or person wholly prosthetic
From bits and pieces of his own,
Displaying his largeness of spirit,
For his heart goes out then to that fiction.
I thicken the gravy then stir it
Silenced by this new conviction

Of understanding, knowing he'll feel
Another mission coming on.
I boil the veg and bin the peel.
He's such a fierce automaton
His breath is steam, his arms are pistons
And what drives him is so inner
It pulls between us such a distance
I dwell on the tastes in my dinner—

All that makes me fully rounded
Slackens my time like detumescence:
All I am is pieces compounded—
Not his hard full single presence
Self-possessed when faced with prostitutes,
Disraeli or Irish angers—
But divergent as my aimless suits
Questioned in the wardrobe by hangers.

A Secret Cyborg

I pecked then hopped, I'd slipped out and blended,
spread my wings and knew I was a sparrow
today as my self extended,
chirping on the handle of a wheelbarrow.

For daily I could feel how I
was more than me, how I ascended
through the veins of the ash into the sky
where all the gaps were mended.

But then my body felt a change
as the thick black thought of the smokestacks
drifted over the hills into my grange
and wafted unseen into my cracks.

There's watts and ohms now in my veins
so part of me dies, this I-morgue
live and wired to others through the mains
becoming a secret cyborg.

My death in life's a cruel sorrow
till I find that I can speed and fly
and plunge into a quick tomorrow,
charged with superpowers I can buy.

Gladstone Speaks from the Afterlife

Hell is other people's memories
Freezing me over
Forever in the same action,

Trapping me in the same frame
Repeated, that contains
Ireland, an axe, a tree

And me, a flat character, the breath
Crushed out of me. I'm shade-thin
In a place that's not a place—

Sun without warmth, flowers without scent,
Music a soundless, head-high
Notation, speech a frozen cloud.

My fingers find
Nothing reciprocal or rough,
Nothing that resists or sticks.

I'm in the landscape where the tunnel starts
And Time the train draws further away
Tightening the frame about me harder and faster.

New Poems I: Heartbreak Hotel

Foreign Bodies

Thirty yards from the violent martyr
I survived, but fragments of the mall
invaded my face and scalp.
A fortnight later, driving to work,
I pictured tweezers at my skin
and thought the headland might feel
the tunnel as a foreign body,
cream cement and steady light and engines
driven through its side.
And I remembered a mosque
converted with statues and portraits,
sandstone breathing alien prayers.
So maybe it was that which grew
the nodule in my nape
my doctor opened up, extracting
a smithereen that she declared
a morsel of the bomber's knee.

Heartbreak Hotel

You're cold and tired and grubby
and struggling to know how to be
when you check into the Heartbreak lobby
to pick up the Heartbreak key.

It's down on Lonely Street
inside a crowded quarter
your past is packed and folded neat
then handed to a porter.

The walls and carpets flash their logo,
sheets, and boxes of matches:
deeply its square tattoo
brands you with its H's.

Straight away you are healing
when that pillow marks your head,
so where there was that feeling
there's a corporate sign instead.

You broach the Heartbreak minibar
to chase away your distress,
peering through a glass of beer
at the Heartbreak trouser-press.

You check out but discover
it's a chain,
you thought you'd erased your lover,
but now you're checking in again:

the vistas diverge and climb
but you wear your brand on your sleeve,
where you can check out any time,
but you can never leave.

Croeso ar Fwrdd Coastliner Cymru

The p.a. voices on the bus concur,
often, in Welsh and English, on the names
of the stops, except the most vernacular,
like Town Ditch in Conwy,
and the bridge in Penmaenmawr,
in Bont Newydd, is deleted
in the English, but they coincide
when it comes to that chapel translated
which is Brookes Tarpaulin.
                                              I enjoy the ride
always: a metal puffin perches
before the Puffin Café, nine feet tall,
the land is mixed use, as though it can't decide,
here—a boarding kennels, silage pouches,
sheep and cows together, it's a spot
you only stop at to refuel,
both voices are silent: railway, culvert
where a stream debouches under the dual
carriageway, unspoken as though covert
or hard to slot into English, like *hwyl*.

When the stops restart, and the voices,
it's the park where the Caravan evolves
into the Cabin, so resolving elsewhere versus
here, with its sea view where limestone dissolves
into islands and headlands. Fixtures
are longed for, but the place has two selves
and I've been thinking all the way from Bangor
of a landscape like those parallel pictures,
Spot the Difference, where the game
involves revealing that a doppelganger
is really not the same.

The Housekeeper

I envy the pre-war dinner-dances in her scrapbook.
Long menus, photos of flushed smilers grouped in evening wear,
the cards that booked her (she was seventeen) for named dances
with gentlemen partners—owners of these spacious, bay-windowed
houses now divided into flats—and their sons, like Kenneth—
how he steps out of the group and smiles alone. And then with her,
engaged. And then in uniform, the RAF, and then
blank pages so I think of him returning to find her
so ancient, pushing a pram the length of the avenue.
He crosses between then and now and suffers the gap
like jetlag, not fitting where it's so much later but he's still
so young: but when I wear her braided broad-shouldered jacket,
coq feathers awry on her small felt hat, it's Kenneth
who watches, who directs the period drama in the mirror,
it's his need invents me as her body double, in her place
whose pram is stuffed with litter and dead leaves like shrivelled faces,
Kenneth latent behind her as in a driver's blind spot,
a streetlamp warming his pallor, where the sycamores
droop with withered fists. I mix another *mojito*,
and sip, and gaze into its drowned vegetation, I'm confused
between before and after, I'm a backseat passenger
who sees in the rearview mirror the green trees
unwinding from the driver's nape: I watch her push the pram
seeing a past that couldn't happen, and leaving
my reflection shuddering in the puddles, all the scene
found wanting, not at all exotic, thirsting to be watched.

Lucky Pierre

The woman kissed me in the club, and her partner
turned and beamed, as pale as a pill a stranger
palms you at 3 a.m., whose name, as the music swells,
is only half heard. I tried to give them the slip,
but they followed me through the riptide of dancers'
elbows and knees into my shoal of slow quiet.

You take the pill to spite yourself for being useless.
Somehow I'd consented beforehand. I was guilty:
Jo the hard cop, Alex the soft, uncovered my taint.
Their hands locked in the small of my back and pressed.

I lay on the sill in the back of their two-seater,
a minus-sign they carried through the icy streets,
we three by contrast with the couples all around us
sleeping and breathing together like a watch sitting
snugly, ticking in time with the pulse below it—
we were mapping a new place, triangulating
beyond the couples who complete each other.

When I woke I was alone in a room where trains
clattered their approach for miles and, only at the last
moment, swerved away, and something hard and stubborn
stuck inside me had been slowly softened and released.
And in the darkness, for hours, faces stuck in lit
windows had been hurtled gawping across my bed.

Desirable Residence

It's 'Bedroom 3', that's 17 x 10,
the one where you could see us through binoculars.
Two windows, telephone point, two double power points,
a radiator. No. We watched you watching,
caught up in its spacious views of trees and sea.
A shower room en-suite, and WC,
sorrento blue, the walls part-tiled. We watched you once
double-glazed through the patio doors, then watched
ourselves in that mirror in the built-in wardrobe.
Daniel: buying this house, what would it solve?
The ceiling's coved. She's lost to us both. Though here
it's 'Bedroom 4', much smaller, 10 x 8,
no phone, a TV point, where we retreated,
sometimes, from the glare. No view, the oaks
hug it close. And in that pile of DVDs,
Goalkeepers From Hell, which features your cock-up
from the Cardiff game, your legs, and then your mouth
are open wide—she loved to watch that, and laughed
hysterically. We shared this phrase—a *safe
pair of hands*—as couples have motifs: the pair she sketched,
and framed on that wall, are smaller, older hands,
they're mine, a haven like this room, where she escaped from yours.
But say you owned the kitchen, all its 17 x 12?
Its antique oak effect cupboards and Aga
where she breathed and thought, but where she isn't now?
She isn't now. What if you wandered through the lounge's
28 x 20, up the stairs, following her steps?
The bedroom you can buy, the time is out of reach—
it's like you'd be condemned to pace forwards and backwards
under the oaks across that soil repeatedly disturbed
where Trish, and her Fluff and Sammy, lie with their heads on their paws.

Dolgarrog Flood, 1925

The church bells woke me, sounding wrong,
too close, too loud, and pealing too late
across the dream I'd caught of Flanders
from my father, muddy meadows,
broken oaks, the trenches awash,
mingled with Dolgarrog when water
smashed our cottage open—as others,
four years later, would be smashed,
when Wall Street crashed—for water,
and no human hand, had rung the bells
of the church, uprooting its nave,
lifting away its graves and altar,
forcing it all downhill
towards our cottage which its hands
turned inside out and emptied
into the cataract that floated
my mattress under the speeding night
towards the aluminium works
whose seven furnaces exploded
adding hell to the high water
where the vicar, fisher of men,
rescued me and sat me on the roof
from where I could see the future
and the past, a village upside down,
the no man's land a shocking force
out of the dark behind our backs
extended miles across the valley,
breaking the fields—the walls and streets
under water, shoes and hats,
a chalice, kettles and legs of chairs,
slowing and sinking as the surface fell.

The Hearing Aid

When you mistake each other or differ,
You worry you'll shrink further from her hearing,
And your words fade, as your wife gets deafer:

Her batteries are flat and she's been left
Insulated with forgotten chairs.
Your beating on the door of the loft

She hears as a small hankering
Confused with memories—
Scratchy tunes, and phrases gone wrong.

The street is at that height where pressure tightens
Before your ears open; a flurry
Of polystyrene settles in flakes, and flattens

Road noises to an echo, padding
Walls with foam; the numbed
Noises in your mouth are clouding—

Each word evaporates
Like skywriting crumbling in the cold.
Your dreaming ears run through their rewrites:

The booth is locked. The lines are down.
The queue lengthens and shakes its fists.
You hold her face in the silent dawn.

The Older Sister

His older sister is so generous.
How he hates the stares men fix on her!

And he dropped in the water a teeming
tissue and forgot to flush and then

his older sister sat herself down
inches above his millions, and now

she's lifting up the neighbour's cat,
her hands pondering the one-year-old

yet sagging belly.
Teeth are growing where her hands press,

claws and pinprick cries, it's like the dark

of a drawer bright with needles,
or a hot night sky

where the white is worming through
the black, a cellar where potato eyes

have grown stalks surrounding her
like a tangle of glances

so she's suddenly a swaying pool
in the top branches of a sycamore

where open mouths are rising
blind and demanding through her dark:

why is it then she's smiling at the cat?

Shrieking Halyards

My thrown white glove is poised
above me in the lights…

Isla, my assistant,
grew too sad for the act
and lives on an arm of land
embracing a cold harbour
sailless yachts congest,
gulls giggling around the bare masts.

The Strait's tides and currents
want to be free, the trapped sea
tears itself apart.

I dwell on the tight huddle
of her like the scented
order of her wardrobe, warm
recesses of her pockets, dark
interior of her pillow,

and my failed dove drops to the stage

Mundane

I
can't
connect
those two
dimensions:
each day I must
repeat my early rising,
the same journey on my bus
to the bags and the bins, the dust,
the same route each week, each day the cart
is only a mile away from the day before, and if I'm ill
it's because I slow down as I fail to see how that can be a part
of the same life that stretches out and out so fast to the far reaches of all
we can see, to Betelgeuse, the supergiant that's burning quite coolly but redly
in winter when I wake in the frost and shiver thinking of the nested dust and gas
shells around it from the mass shrinking from it over aeons. In such a deadly
climate even my thought can't breathe for long. I am a dustman but
it's difficult even to get dressed and butter my toast sometimes
when awe slows me at the dust that burst out as a star lit
a billion alien skies for weeks only and fused together
and I feel the planet orbit instead of the carpet
under my feet, because that start won't fit
with how it led to now, this weather,
my lounge—it narrows further
to my sofa where a steep
gravity opens a drop
inside, so I slow
further—I slow
much further
to a full
stop
.

World of Interiors

the thick wool please
and not the cumulonimbus thankyou with ice in its head,
its crystals and breath that forces higher pretending
it's solid until you're falling and its rooms are rushing
through your fingers

the short days please
the shut blinds
the walls warming
and not the estuary thankyou opening and opening
as though it could unwind me out of myself and scatter me
into the widening dissolve of those lanes where you could look up
soaked through, soaked, at the liner towering above you
but so close in your water you can hear its engines clattering

the hot bath please,
the steamed tiles

and not the helicopter tiny between the steep
towers of flickering glass which fails to hold the nimbus
scattering or the rain opening and closing its stretched
partitions

please, please,
the hot water bottle, sheets
and mattress that enfold

and not the gusts that scatter thank you and shift the brutal
sunlight that insists on the broken glass in neglected corners
and lots not far from the buses and pavements
where women are weeping into their phones

a burrow please, a mute tunnel,
fur and rabbit breath, the shared
warmth of close bodies, or perhaps

a night in one of those hotels
in Tokyo where you can dig yourself
inside a cupboard with a bed inside.

Box of Vision

But if he came for me the camera would see:
it watches Market St., the railings and buses,
the three approaches to my first-floor flat,
and knows the shifts, the bustling hours and the quiet,
fixing its one unsleeping dry or rain-streaked eye
on paving and macadam, two trees, a streetlight
—would catch his shadow hunching across the road,
his leaning silhouette against the railings
where the camera's vision ends, before the park
that stretches beyond its cramped ken into pathways
through the darkness of the copse and boatless lake,
too deep and far in for the camera which is content
with its lot, and never sees the sun or moon
but watches shadows grow and shrink, and windscreens flash,
and holds each detail tight in its memory: paint
drying on the railings, how it chips and cracks, and paint
drying again, then rain and heat and dust on paint
that chips and cracks, and could rewind the painting
and drying, and play it back in slow motion,
and captures him there as one of many objects
in its field, where nothing escapes its eye
and total recall: I envy its security
of knowing it all, and wish I too could let
shifts of light and traffic wash across my bounded sight,
could climb inside its box of vision where the weather
falls into my open eyes, and figures cross in crowds
and one might stand and stare, but never can enter
the zone of comfort where I watch this space

The Breasts

Her breasts had secretly acquired
an agent, knowing they were better
than their owner—when she tired
and sagged, they only perked up perter,
climbing above her. She had made it
only because they stood up for her,
who always denied them credit
for parting the way before her.
Now they needed to expand
their contract: they'd get bigger
only if they could command
a much more generous figure.
Oh my God I'm falling apart
she cried, awaking in the cold dawn:
tired of being tied to a tart,
and haughty about her soft porn,
they slipped away to a new start
with others of their sharp design
that strives towards a stern ideal
of rational form, of taut hard line,
with creatures cool in their glass, their steel
and tubular chrome, who can appeal
to cyborg longings to combine
in webs with perfect clones, where one
hears their thoughts and is never alone.

The breasts were secretly admired
by many for how they simplified
their roles, and they were hired
by many directors who relied
on how each time they could enact
a potent truth that stayed the same,
supplying what the public lacked,
and that ensured their growing fame.

Emily Dickinson Updates Her Facebook Status

I heard this bug, and then the light
totally crashed and now I'm like—

Spar Radio

Something Tanya said,
and this singer's anger
and pain, and French bread
bristling at the aisle end.
I'm hollow with hunger.

Tanya said it won't mend.
They won't—those chocolate fingers—
fill me up for long.
Tanya would hate this song
but share the singer's

throaty shout of wrong.
The breakfast cereal aisle
can feel her lips and tongue,
breathes with her lungs and heart.
A guilty denial

unnerves me by the fridge,
whose loveless weather
penetrates my shirt.
Yes: milk and porridge.
The throwing together

of passion spent and shopping
strands me by the cold meats
and fish, just gawping
as the singer eats
her heart out,—it's so raw

to hear that singer
grunt, as though she's liable
to weep on the store's floor—
it's so exposed, so raw
as though your offhand rough finger
brushed your own eyeball.

The Cu Chi Tunnels

The actor dressed as Vietcong lowered himself
agilely down the tiny hole, so that the sod
on top of his helmet fitted so perfectly
into its mouth the hole vanished and the ground healed,
and I was thinking of that evening you talked about
power—how, between us, it was me who was
powerful. Straight away you took that back, but power
is often on your mind and I could see you thinking
about a tiny people retreating into tunnels,
knowing you were small and ginger and bullied
as a child and learned then how to fight your battles
secretly, and here a people fought against its fat
oppressors by hiding where gigantic bulk
excluded their asses, left them to tower in the open
where they could be struck, as if a rabbit could
ambush an eagle. How you smiled, identifying,
because at work you order your bailiwick
sensing the nearness of threats like a submarine
that's tracking you on its radar, threats persisting
always, as though you're powerless. And under our marriage
you've dug a network of tunnels like a tangle
of rope, and I am cumbersome, gigantic,
hobbled by the rope entangling my ankles.

The Stuffing Boxes

I love those words but often I can't grasp
their live load: *Harry saw the young
Cuban smile in the binnacle light*—
the novelist, who knows such names,
has sometimes thought inside their weft,
has skippered boats or broken wild horses.
Reading you detect distraught sinew,
muscle in despair you're sure
they must've felt, and access opened
where the gate is normally padlocked
at the bridge to the landscaped island.
So you're half on, half off that boat
where Harry puts one hand on the
water manifold, the cylinders
and then the stuffing boxes, and the cloud
reflected in the water keeps
receding so your boat can never
enter the patch where it sits.
And yet it's marvellous to embark
and also know I needn't stay
on board, and watch my train shift
the setting west of Abergele,
seeing the coast off Cienfuegos,
Harry tightening the grease cups
a turn and a half each.

The Prison of Memory, 1989

Two decades ago the Red Square Parade
On *News at Ten* got mingled with my saunter -
Fretting about what makes us afraid -
Towards this vast white concrete remand centre.
First, because I strolled up from behind,
I saw its fenced-in tip: old mattress,
Box and broken chair before a fortress
Like a Freudian symbol of the anxious mind.

The worry of one in this connection
Presses from without, the other from within,
Which hints how fever for protection
From without can alter minds and turn us in—
As though away from sleet, denial
Hunching our heads, or doubting our innocence,
Insinuating an obscure offence,
Until we feel remanded, pending trial.

The times now interact, and the places—
New light on the bone-white elm, the green
Chain-mail of the chestnuts, tight maces
Where their tall flowers withdrew, the too-hot scene
Swells with too much meaning: *Danger* signs
I hardly noticed grow out of proportion
Round the rubbish, I'm nostalgic for a caution
I grew up with, and not along the new lines

Complicating the scene. The old condition
Lures me back, I watch again the bolted doors,
Look through the barred windows of transition.
If the prisoners' crimes were cancelled, and the laws
All changed one day, the warders disappeared
And gates opened, some would slip out straight away,
But some would pull the doors shut and stay,
Insisting their cases must be heard.

Breaking the Ice

Your fretting about the welfare
of the whole planet jars between us.
I charge across the surface to brace myself for
spinning high above the ice.
We're skating on a lovely day.
The star that starts to shine is Venus
but you say what shines is sulphur,
Venus shines through acid clouds.
My love of fun you say is just display.
You giggle. Yes. You like my style.
I leap and spin a pirouette
on ice that's shining like a smile
below that scorched erotic star.
The breeze adores us it's so wet
so warm the ice begins to sweat.
I've pushed beyond—it's like a drive
to twist this frenzied spin,
to spin at the top
of my leap, I'm so alive
I'm infectious: you can't stop
yourself from joining in.

The Gold Bar

I threw a gold bar off the pier once.

On his death bed Peter Evans said this to Tony Abbott who's staring at the stretch of water where the gold must've lodged. The low December sun confuses the eye with silhouettes and patches of glare. He spots, half the pier away, the approaching Geraint Williams—co-conspirator with Peter in notorious practical jokes.

Tony is in bad debt and imagines learning to be a frogman and diving for the ingot. He said to the dying Peter that God would still welcome him because he'd always been such a good man. Peter had once given him a sofa and a dishwasher, and he would visit Tony in his terraced house and talk about his anxieties about his son, and other sensitivities that weren't evident when he and Geraint were surrounded by their laughing cronies in the pub. Tony felt excluded from that, but the confession was quiet, like their one-to-one conversations—Peter had slipped the bar off a trolley where it was sitting with a hundred others, but then he'd felt guilty and afraid.

Sad about Peter, Geraint says.

Very sad.

The pier ends in rusty steps with barbed wire and a *Keep Out* sign. The sea surface is dazzled by the oblique sun.

Even near the end he was worried about your debt.

If a pier's a disappointed bridge, this one's especially frustrated: it reaches out from Bangor and ends only five hundred yards short of Anglesey.

Sports Psychology

No-one at his club who mattered would believe that lost love was a serious injury. He was a very promising left-sided centre-half and had represented England at Under-21 level and was starting to establish his place in the Tottenham side. But the tackle that Sienna had inflicted, although he was 1.93 metres and 74 kg., had flattened him like a kick to his cruciate ligament delivered so swiftly that a camera could only detect it in slow motion. The photos that his private detective sent him on WhatsApp showed him what was up. Which he had guessed because Sienna still slept with him but much less often and their conversations now were halting and betrayed lack of interest by both of them. He was queasy inside his six-pack: he didn't pine for *this* Sienna but for the woman he had thought she was, who didn't exist. In the moment which has been repeatedly replayed on television he was badly out of position. Seconds before the Stoke left-back fired in a cross with vicious swerve and dip, he had been frozen by an image from a year before of a slight quiver of Sienna's lips as they parted from his own. Just after their striker, in two metres of shockingly free space, headed the ball in the net, he stood on the penalty spot, in the terrible din of crowd outrage, feeling a deep sense of futility.

Muntjak

I hated the deer because, when I found her under my apple tree, she had the eyes of a homeless beggar. I hated her appeal of fur and warm blood.

When my marriage was collapsing we fumigated the house three times trying to delete the cat fleas, but they were relentless. All over my body there was a terrible itch and, when I finally took refuge with a friend, I felt guilty that I would contaminate his sofa and his spare bed.

Just before I abandoned the marital home I let a contact lens slip from my fingers down the sink. I found it under the drainpipe lodged in the ooze and matted hair like a fingernail in a pie of human meat. No matter how much I cleaned it I couldn't bring myself to slot it in my eye because of what it had seen on its journey down the moist tube.

I wish I was one of the super-rich in Sao Paolo who travel only by helicopter above the teeming streets.

When I first moved to this house I watched three cats staring at a slowworm they had sliced up, staring at its three components wriggling. From time to time the ginger middle one reached out its paw to test one of the agonized segments.

In the early hours last night I woke realising I'd forgotten to empty the vacuum cleaner and worried it contained living ants like the Underground mass of jostled bodies which get squirted out into the streets under pressure from the tubes.

A stranger is seated next to me on my sofa. Her blood has the scent of hot iron, or soil aroused by a tropical sun.

Fluent

So what my body had performed by itself before I was forced now to achieve by conscious effort. I needed to speak to my body in its difficult language. I needed to remember all the kinds of flow and where they were and what directions they must follow and how they all needed to keep going at once. I almost, early on, forgot the chyme. The limbic system resented my rational control and tried to blockade its fornix to subvert my transmissions. Distracted, I almost forgot to replace the red blood cells and panicked because the word *erythropoiesis* escaped me. Certain involuntary muscles and reflex actions like swallowing insisted on their autonomy.

Gradually, however, I pulled myself together. I quelled all opposition and directed my messages to every part, knowing with the flow as I extended everywhere. I was thoroughly in charge.

Then I was top-down managing and flowing through the atoms in the cells and adjusting the electrons with my microfingers, so many, so very many, manipulating the charge and propelling the molecules across the membranes, until I was released from my enclave into a larger cavity. From there I entered an opening where the metaphors tumbled away like ladders under my feet so I knew the branches and vessels and walls and pathways for what they are.

And then my knowing opened further and wider and further until I knew I could command the gaps between brains and link them so together through our knowing of our minds we could encompass all that lived between them and beyond.

Glass Houses

They startled me at first, the stones hitting my house, I thought that someone had climbed onto my roof. The first one struck just before ten o' clock one evening when I was cleaning my teeth and winding down towards an early night. It hit just under the bathroom window where I was standing, so I wondered if the perpetrator had seen my silhouette. The next night, at just after two in the morning, a stone smashed my bedroom window. I was upset because the glass was Victorian and slightly shimmered here and there with beautiful flaws, and I disliked replacing it with double glazing.

After a week they started to feel like something that was bound to happen, and appropriate, which I deserved, and a half-articulate mode of communication. They began not long after I was acquitted, about six months after the accident. They mostly happened at night, mostly, so they got muddled up with my sleep. They always felt as though hurled across a great divide, like a parallel universe trying to speak to me: I wanted to be able to reply in the same baffled language, somewhere in the boundary between music and noise. Sometimes, though, I felt vertiginously anxious about interpreting them like this and not as simple dangerous aggression.

It's been over a year now since the bombardment started, and the local newspaper has reported it under the headline 'Great Catapult Mystery', describing the culprit as a 'mysterious catapult fiend who unleashes a barrage of tennis-ball size missiles only at night'. The report added that the North Wales police have failed to find the fiend despite using 'the entire might of modern police methods, from infra-red cameras to detectives hiding under the bushes'. The police asked a ballistics expert from Bangor University to attempt to pinpoint the catapult by working out the trajectory and speed of the missiles. They also asked the parish priest, the Rev. Colin Williams, if it might be a poltergeist that was hurling the stones, but he replied, impatiently, that this was not a case for exorcism.

I woke just now, feeling the impact of the stone under my window like a blow just under my ribs and remembering my Volvo that night hitting the darkly-clad old woman who had stepped into the unlit rural road.

Socialism for the Rich

Hot mergers were the driving force for Charles Wheeler, and his numbers were astonishing, but we knew he was burning himself up inside. Everyone in the City felt his influence, he was massive and he radiated vast amounts of heat and light. Others were drawn to him and circled around him, glowing with his reflected brilliance. They caught his linguistic habits, his unique way of talking. Where others would have said 'Shit happens', he said 'Entropy increases'. When a burnt-out colleague retired, he referred to his 'exit velocity'.

He was consuming himself, depleting his energy, and he started to collapse under the drag of his own enormity. The Government stepped in and attached him to the National Grid, to try to hold him up. Our lights flickered, and then our power shut off for hours. We were left in the dark. But it was no use and he was soon extinguished.

There was consternation, and amazement, when he simply vanished. 'Abducted by aliens', Olivia said, and we all nervously laughed. It was hard to keep your feet on the ground, there was a groundswell. Others were soon vanishing as well, and we noticed, in the corridor that led to Wheeler's office, a terribly powerful force that sucked you towards his door. People were saying that Wheeler was still around, like a ghost, and devouring people more literally than before.

Today I noticed a violent interference in the space between the cash register in Café Nero and the espresso machine, a fluctuation of sudden and very high frequency, and it sucked in a trainee barista and then my accountant friend Matt, just as he was balancing a carton of water on his tray next to the steaming mugs.

Where will it end?

New Poems II:
The Slasher and the Vampire
as Role Models

You Faithless Slime

The number whose call I missed
was 666-666-666.
The devil does exist:
that *thing* upstairs is not my phone
and suddenly *Tubular Bells*
has made itself my ring tone
and it rang and then the bed
below it shook, and voicemail said
the point is to make you despair.
The devil does exist
and entered my phone as malware
when I googled *The Exorcist,*
and threatened my very sim.
A billion Catholics might lapse
with their networks tangled in sin
and a virus tormenting their apps
when their devices pass this meme on,
swiftly across desks and deep into laps,
mutating like a demon.

Outlaws

Night chill, and red heat far as the day stretches,
desert rocky and high, beyond all laws,
coyotes somewhere, thin air, apaches,
and the tall man easy on the brisk horse.

I used to think I drove the wild route
like this of a secret outsider.
Lofty in my big truck, a charming brute.
Alert while others slept, an easy rider.

Out on the edges of your sleep I steered
through badlands all my own, concealed frontiers
in England like a dream trail I pioneered —
until the weight of civilised English years

closed around me like dripping viney elms.
I lost a freedom I could never own,
the landscape stretching out of U.S. films.
The wary stranger in the wooden town

trots in from a place so open to question
maps can only guess, and so unfenced and raw
that any minute in the shifting Western
the lawman changes into the outlaw.

But rails and blocked roads are knotted tight
across these midlands rotting with wet heat.
I feel I must've tensed up for a gunfight
then fallen with a foot wound writhing in defeat.

Or I'm a fridge that's off: inside me, mince
warms and turns — because the English air is thick
with used-up thoughts and dust from crowded skins.
But in the glove compartment my sidekick

chambers its bullets safely. It's fated.
Scorching in this lane I doze in my cab
and clingy branches crowd me. I've mutated
like a virus released from a lab:

the bullets, bursting from that steel grip, will see,
beyond their blur of speed, the big change, and pierce
through to where they turn a fierce key
that opens England up with weird frontiers.

Major Lawrence

for Steve Ormrod

I wipe the film from my gasmask's lenses,
peering towards the flaring horizon
where a Scud's slipped through our Patriot defences,
but the fireworks fuzz in the lenses' scratches.
Lawrence with his Arab disguise on
is with me often, and how Lean lingers
on desert stretches like a flaring pain
expanded of the safety matches
snuffed out by O'Toole on his fingers,
as though what drove that Arab campaign
was Lawrence's epic sickness and need,
divided as the loudspeakers on poles
around us broadcasting Scud alarms
but also calls to prayer. Contrasting roles —
a scholar inflicting guerrilla harms,
determined that the Arabs be freed,
but serving first the British empire.

How I hate the hot pissy aura
he hated of squaddies *en masse* —
a major feeling minor, I disappear,
I'm ghostly and anonymous
inside the ranks of scientific killers
and the shimmering sky and sand of the Gulf,
thinking of Lawrence naming flora
and rocks, inhabiting his Seven Pillars,
drawing on war to express himself
and looming like David Lean as director
of himself, so large in the bigger picture.

I shrink inside my charcoal-lined jacket.
I'm contained between my helmet and rubber boots
bumping along one of the routes
we've bulldozed out of the desert, sick
of airborne poisons and the racket,
both sides vying for spoils—
and pine for a dishdasha, and rafiq
to lead me to a ruined desert palace
whose clay was kneaded with essential oils
so I could understand, in Arabic,
each room with its own scent of jessamine,
of violet or of rose. The Seven Pillars
glowing at sunset at sandstone Wadi Rum
echoed to him like a high muezzin.
Lean has Lawrence say the desert's clean,
that's why he loves it. Now the sands swarm
with littered bunkers, canvas with mildew,
redolence of piss and feet and Vietnam,
the TV crews composing a scene.

How many times I've willed you,
Lawrence of Arabia, to defy the norm
Of class and empire. I have been you,
seizing Aqaba, where you diminish
and hate yourself for being cruel,
rejecting honours and spoils,
and push beyond the loss of self in action—
eating green dates and camel sinew,
loving the desert like a holy fool,
rejecting even rooms scented with essential oils
in favour of that pure
breath of the scentless desert wind, to punish
yourself with rarefaction,
and push beyond to taste
that absence of scent in an air
throbbing out of endless miles of scorched waste.

Being Requited

The suit and tie of Cary Grant,
and how, when forced to run, he carries his cuffs
deep into the tall corn, then coughs
inside a cloud of crop dust—this is all I want
to picture of a way to be and look.
And when I ached with teenage fuzz
of being—dither and the body's hot scuzz—
his suave composure filled my lack.

Ugly and gauche I prayed to his icon
blu-tacked above my bed, and plotted revenge
for being ignored. I forced a change:
I had no style but learned to fake one,
and sharpened my doubtful edges
into the focus of a fixed role—
as though my fear had grown unreal,
or turned into tenth-storey window ledges

I blithely sauntered over—or been laughed
away because I learned to play me
like that screwball Grant in *Bringing Up Baby*,
winning Hepburn just by being daft.
Except I always felt unsuited,
dazed like someone always called the wrong name,
and haunted everywhere by blame.
How come I was so persecuted?

Watch me turn from where the corpse collapsed.
The knife was glinting in my hand.
The cameras flashed, onlookers gasped
and none of us could comprehend...
But I suspect myself: it's me, the danger
climbing stairs, my debonair disguise on,
bearing a glass of milk that glows with poison,
but blankly staring. It's my anger

scares me now I'm suave and handsome,
so I ponder (charged with new power)
that lacking conquests then, in ugly despair,
I stayed at home and violently planned some.
I'm the hero: stretching flat land behind me
looks towards me where the camera praises
my habit of attracting gazes—
watch me draw a plane out of the sky to find me

but I'm sickened by too much success
and pushed beyond the bounds of plenty
into a landscape dry and empty
because I'm drained by such excess
of what was once too much denied.
My self's deleted by my stage name.
I overflowed too far into fame,
requiting wants that leave a need

for the one blonde to run with in the wood
towards a climax where it's all explained
and all that happened was all planned,
we're getting married and I turn out good.
Suited and excited in a high place
I know myself at last, this new man:
here, it's all so meaningful and human
every crag is bulging with a vast face.

The Living Dead

When dawn is early, in summer, the city centre
resembles those pictures I've carried with me so long
they're like a place that must exist somewhere, an after
time when trees have taken over, or reptiles: zombies
stumble manically through the malls and squares, and then
the cities are nearly vacant, except the crevices
burgeon inside their concrete and tarmac with mutant
seeds and insects too resilient ever to die.
But now the networks persist: I know I'm being filmed
as I gather my nest of blankets by the bank,
wincing from a phrase inside me like a twinge
in a Cardiff accent, bossy and scornful, then
a German snigger: I'm *infected* as if a flue
out of a mall, a draught from an alley, crack
in a pavement, planted a whisper only
some of us hear, who sleep with our ears to the ground,
a broken phrase from a voiceover, foretelling
a purge when the planet will be cured of its crowds
and turn its cleared face again to the starlight
whose voices have been waiting so long out of earshot.

A Police Officer Called Marilyn

My mother adored Monroe
and called me Marilyn.
My father's talk was faith and sin
and they were always in a row.
He ended as Chief Constable.

Sometimes I woke and thought the house spoke
desire ghostly as the smell of smoke,
or a wriggly elusive mouse:
scurryings and scratchings that trouble
the silence at the dinner table.

Mother looked up from *Niagara*
awed by the power of Monroe's allure,
claimed dad was a useless ogre.

Guiltily, I was drawn to the law.

I worked in Vice as though I was immune
for years before I felt what Vice was for.

I hate these cravings. Hate it that they're mine:

they shimmer my familiar outline
and discover I'm my mother's double,
in conflict with my boss, the Chief Constable.

I should diet, try some new exercises.

How sharp it is—Gerald's stubble.

I sit at my desk and feel unable
and longings creep in like the slow dark
across the meadows mined with warrens,
over the ring road, through the high rises,
over the waste ground's fireweed and rubble,
through the subways like desire and the empty park,
and the hungry hollows fraught with sirens.

My husband's shrewd detective's eyes
observe me in our bed and bath.
He's dirty from a cruel shift
searching the common and the woods,
a weedy, demented garden path.

I manage two unwary lies.
I'm sleepy under the slippy suds,
trembly and flickering as a bubble,
silly and adrift.
He notes my frown, distracted laugh.
He mustn't notice Gerald's stubble
touchily inflames my chin and inner thighs.

Gerald's fridge-magnet Marilyn
has seven outfits.
                    I undress her,
it's a slow and calm pleasure
to stroke the yearned-for skin
of the plastic idol.
Naked, she's a scared creature out of its shell,
too quivering-raw and white,
and all a blonde muddle
troubling her charismatic glow.

Naked, she's a cloud, Monroe,
a cloud your plane is rising through—
the windows flicker: she's this glow
you reach all shuddery in your levelled flight.

I need to drop the discipline
my dad imposed, so Marilyn
is with me: she's the saint
of knowing how to live with unrestraint,
I have to follow what she knows
but not that image stalely
bigging up the norms
of Jack's and Tony's horns:
I have to follow Monroe's
example, not that little ukulele.

Still I recoil from the sinful taint.

I falter, hesitating
like a shy girl trying to flirt.

Millions of thoughts alight on Marilyn's body.
The breeze from the subway grating
lifts her as it lifts her skirt—

I see her rising higher like a saint
towards heaven, but drunkenly unsteady.

A Dentist's Jane Austen

I wear, in most of my secluded hours,
An elegant dress out of Gainsborough;
I play piano, stitch my tapestry flowers,
Unfold to my sister or my mirror
Passion otherwise concealed where surfaces
Uphold the daily ceremony,
On weekdays and the sabbath, which services
The needs of older and more recent money.

It's oh so soothing to find myself lost in
A family in a village: ingenue,
Learning, blooming, in a film of Jane Austen
Hoarding my secret in my bed or my pew,
With so much meaning packed in tight, compact,
Inside a single parish, plot of ground
Whose lanes and houses and gardens interact
With women, and the men for whom they're bound

Unlike, outside my surgery, the street
Which can't contain itself, but must extend
To roads and motorways, is incomplete
Forever, opens outwards without end
Transforming as it widens into stretches
Ever further beyond my comprehension.
On that set, instead, the prospect of riches
Grips the familiar vista in a tension

Mounting from what's observed and what ignored.
The candles glint on Wedgewood—I can see
Moody shadows hurt the brow of the lord
Who wants me in secret in the Regency.
My sister whispers guesses. We confide
But motives flicker as in candlelight.
The present comes to me and opens wide,
Its tongue is on display. The guilty delight

Is missing of masking and unmasking
Except my mask which fends away bacteria.
Shopping with my small daughter, multi-tasking,
Even then, I'm drawn to the deeper interior
Where I'm tense with looming disclosures:
Faces at the masked ball are hidden
As my work-bag hides its knives and scissors.
From my window then, I notice—sudden

Too sudden, as though the village wore a mask
It then removed—the changes have begun
Where a formal, stable scene might ask
How it contains already its own
Undermining. What the scene was hiding
Coins an altered language, joins the new fashion:
Like a pained lover down the lanes comes riding
An era with a solemn voice, a sad passion.

Meg Ryan

My girlfriend wanted a rom com.
I wanted action or a zom one
with our takeaway, the lamb
bhuna and chicken tikka. A time bomb
between us had ticked since the tom tom
I bought on her birthday. Not much rom
between us, she said. And not much com
either I replied. We couldn't com
-promise. She frisbeed her poppadom
at my head and now she's gone.

The Porter and the Slasher

I am a caring person,
and my trolley is immaculate.

My sheets and blanket are clean and neat.

But a blade—or a house
an ancient tribe has put a curse on—
or a knife, or an axe, arouse
me against my will

and when I'm wheeling a person
who is very unwell
I'm quiet and attentive—I

am far from those scenarios
where anyway I always identify
with youths the slasher chose
to punish.
         My low-key tasks
nonetheless help to save lives
while all around me men in masks
are wielding their clever knives.

A knife that catches the light on screen
can seem to open like a mouth
that's trying hard to mean
a painful but urgent truth,

how no-one can conquer evil,
how it's back each time, so youth
must suffer its revival,
must atone for a wrong that's ancient,

and I cast myself in that cursed place—
I'm wheeling a patient
groggy after her op,
but fighting that primordial force,
the slasher no-one can stop,
who sometimes, however, wears my face.

Off the Road

Five days we've hid inside while it has snowed,
and watched the news of snow, and cars forced
on hard shoulders—and his box set
with all those prairies that exhaust
my husband, brief motels and then the road
again, the highway always, straight between the wheat,
the highway that continues till it's lost,
the sofa like his passenger seat.

There isn't one of us who doesn't itch
for newness, for a strange departure,
who doesn't want to hitch
herself into an open future,
and envies those U.S. actors who've chosen
the changing and difficult, while all
our nation's traffic grid is frozen.

But through the smoke from a new spliff
that clouds the screen, my husband hears a call
(although it doesn't raise him from his back)—
the road's a cunning temptress, noir
and sunset-red and shimmery-elusive,
enough to drive him from our cul-de-sac,
enough if only he could choose, if
only he weren't hitched, his car
dragging a fat slow trailer,
house and wife and child—he won't get far
without his TV and his dealer,

though he hankers to be driven to the Point
of No Return, to whisper with the Femme
Fatale, to drink with the Taciturn Killer
and the Drifter who's being tailgated
by a demon.
                Now he stares into his joint,
the scorched sunset at its tip, frustrated
like he's spent a fortnight in a traffic jam,
that even on that movie road are stops
where he must linger, stalled and deflated—
and he longs to go careering like a pram
plunging down a hundred stone steps.

Bishop Shoots Brando

The young man heading towards his first hit
can feel that he is dangerous.
The New York night is hot,
aghast with watching windows, and his gun
trembles from his holstered heart.
Finding himself will strike him like a loss.

It's sinful that I think of this again
and again, and wrong that I interpret
these pastries as too highly wrought,
neurotic corn dollies, tortured raffia,
these offerings at the Women's Bazaar
as though they all unveil a secret —

it isn't theirs, it's *my* desire
that colours with suspicion all I see
and draws me to the Catholic heat
and terrible glamour of the Mafia:
daily routines of mutual hurt,
all so unlike the kind old C of E

where drizzle is dampening all my see.
At long inductions under my mitre
I long to love and hate
and feel the tensions of *omerta*,
dwelling on codes that disagree
with all my conscience tells me to be.

Forgive me. It's my wicked double —
torn by guilt like God's commando —
who pulls a gun out of his chasuble
and shoots Pacino, de Niro and Brando.
I shun my wife, consult my lonely heart:
I've done, then, all I *can* do.

The Process

There's a frame, if you freeze it, where Russell Crowe
is stepping backwards as though I've scared him.
I enter these epics in their margins
and so briefly I'm a blur in the crowd,
and only ever seen, so even my phone,
chirping under my chainmail, goes unheard.
I spoke a line once, but didn't like it,
and preferred being back in the ranks, an army,
one of those masses on screen that are watched
from above so they resemble cloud breaking
apart and undulating, or the flatness
suddenly of a broad river as it nears
a waterfall, and which implies that history
is a wave and not a particular hero.
Playing a part in that, to be inside
the process, an enzyme, almost impossible
to see, alongside so many others,
that I love, that hidden making of change.

The Familiar

The foreign owners won't promote me
and I took my revenge with a joke
that started from the pale beauty
of the son, his drained bewildered look
of a modish vampire whose need
appalls him—that he's so confined
inside an alien drive to feed
it sickens his sense of his own kind.

The old one looks like Christopher Lee
and founded far away (they're Serbs)
the highly respected company.
He lives on the threshold where suburbs
succumb to woodland: overgrown,
his garden lets it in behind.
In front his stern old gables frown
on the traffic and ephemera,
the rooms are shakily confined
inside a lost subjective camera
that's taken hold of my eyes
and leads me down his passageways...

in early twilight, late December,
past their windows numb with ice,
I'm led by hand to that hot chamber
hoping to change as the solstice
nudges open the year's door,
hoping there they might dismember
all my sameness of before,
unlock me at my throat
and let my poisons flood
from me, until I can devote
myself by freeing my bad blood.

I know I must be wrong to rebel.
I'm only jealous of their clique.
They pay me and they're right to compel
me when I'm overturned by pique.

I want those two to quell my demons,
cut me down to the quiet size
of a creature drawn by their summons
struggling through the thickened light,
a creature who so much denies
itself it falters out of sight,
on its frail wings.
      For I unnerve
myself with wrong thoughts, and might
find peace inside that role, discover
I can fit what I deserve
by handing myself completely over.

The Foreign Secretary Circles the Wagons

The pictures are so puerile I grimace.
Sometimes even in Parliament:
the rocky desert shimmers
and the hero's virile extent
is measured by the cameras
panning to the red arroyo.

Maybe an unconscious ploy though
reminds me of the sandstone ledge
he tiptoes over, flattening his chest —
to point to how on edge
they were, extending the driven West,
and show, foreshadowed in that mirror,
dimlit extras behind our back
conspire and frame relentless terror.

Vibrant arrows strike the frail shack:
the pictures rise up from a known
compartment of how I think, their shock
arises from their being my own.

I'm startled by the radio alarm —
its voice inside me as I woke
as though it was my dream that spoke
my name, and said I was naive.
I'm under siege. I've lost the charm
I hid behind. The press
is groping for holes in my defences.

Bullets shatter the shack,
each way I swivel they can see my back;
the windows explode, the floorboards heave.
I'm hit and prey to a thousand fancies,
each time I speak I falter and digress.

And no-one can be a hero
now there's no action, all the best
subject to relentless opinion

and I slip around in my role
as though the stagecoach I'm locked inside
has lost its driver to an arrow
and the horses out of control
plunge towards the edge of the canyon—

but when, again, I glance outside,
it's drizzly-green and dim with mist:
I'm hurtling through an English countryside.

Unearthly Hour

In deepest space the thinking species
are reptiles and insects who converse
by throwing their thoughts. You feel this voice
burning like shame or fizzing like fun:
the breeze, where no human race is,
stinks with thought beneath their queasy sun—

which shrinks now to a distant star
(although my nostrils hold that smell
my bedroom fug could not dispel)
as I stumble out to my car
on call, and, while I crunch the gravel,
hear that whisper ravel

inside the copse, the undercurrent
of the hidden stream
like thinking that runs in parallel
to what we know, a nearby variant
we can't suspect—or muffled scream
of someone shipwrecked in the hell

of a frozen and murky planet.
I'm alone on these rural roads
and then—I can't explain it—
my voices start. I know they're wrong,
not even there, like creepy codes
inside our thoughts that don't belong

but slip inside us like bacteria.
We're aliens to ourselves, disown
the landscape of our own interior:
livid tunnels, urgent streams, the nerves
and organs—ours and yet unknown,
terrain inside us that unnerves

our sense of what we are.
My voices turn me inside out,
each alien message places
the edges of my self in doubt—
my boundaries thin and stretch so far
that I dissolve into those spaces

where I'm lost, as now. I stop the car—
my patient's house was here. It's gone.
The darkness moves things. I'm alone
as though I fell out of the sky,
silenced because I feel bizarre,
that nothing around me can comply

with how it strikes me, and I hum
with alien transmissions, beeps and eeks,
the stark surprise of how my thought speaks—
suspicion, guess, this inkling,
surprising me they're mine, who's dumb,
but talked at by the dark's twinkling.